BRUISED BUT NOT broken

Sydney & Lisa,
You may be bruised but you are NOT broken!

XO
Jenne

#BruisedButNotBrokenBook

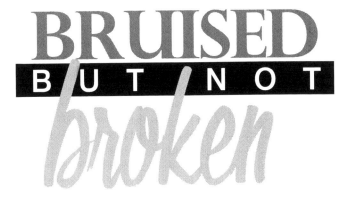

TORRIE CHATMAN

Bruised but Not Broken

Copyright © 2016 by Torrie Chatman Enterprises, LLC.

ISBN 978-1-53330-182-6

All rights reserved. No portion of this book may be reproduced, stored in a retrieval system, or transmitted in any form or by any means, except for brief quotations in printed reviews, without prior permission of Torrie Chatman. Requests may be submitted by email: contact@torriechatman.com.

Permission notices for the lyrics that appear in chapter nine and chapter sixteen are listed on page 173, which hereby becomes a part of this copyright page.

This book recounts events in the life of Torrie Chatman according to the author's recollection and perspective. Some names and details have been changed to protect the privacy of individuals.

Front cover design by Chantee Jackson.

Photography by Eric Dejuan.

Editing by *www.ChristianEditingServices.com*.

www.torriechatman.com

This book is dedicated to two of the greatest loves of my life, Jessica and Mama.

Our path didn't look like anyone else's, and for that I'm appreciative. It made us who were destined to be. I wouldn't trade our bond, trials, victories, or love for anything in this world.

Jessica, you are strong, beautiful, and gifted. Very few understand me the way you do. Thank you for hearing the unspoken words of my heart and being one of my biggest cheerleaders and greatest inspirations. I love to love you. You keep me connected, silly, and innovative. I'll never give up on you or all you have to offer this world. It's your time to shine, baby girl!

Michelle Denise McClamb, you were known to so many as a nurse, sister, friend, daughter, Tupac's greatest fan, and the infamous "Bombshell." Jessica and I are grateful to have known you as our mama! Your sacrifices were endless and your love is now eternal. Every day of your life, you not only told but also showed us that you wanted us. I'm thankful you taught and gave us all you had. Your legacy lives on through your babies. I hear your voice every time I laugh, see your smile every time I look in the mirror, and feel your heart beat whenever I place my hand on chest. Your love has made me everything I am today.

MTJ123
Michelle, Torrie, and Jessica. We were always meant to be. This book is for us.

Rest in heaven, Mommy!

Contents

	Foreword	9
	Introduction	13
1	This Woman's Work —*Kate Bush*	15
2	M!ssunderstood —*P!nk*	23
3	Fallin' —*Alicia Keys*	29
4	Love is Blind —*Eve*	35
5	Nobody Knows —*P!nk*	45
6	Ex-Factor —*Lauryn Hill*	55
7	Don't You Forget It —*Glenn Lewis*	69
8	You Gotta Be —*Des'ree*	77
9	Imagine Me —*Kirk Franklin*	87
10	Golden —*Jill Scott*	93
11	Lately —*Stevie Wonder*	101
12	Gravity —*John Mayer*	109
13	Gone Already —*Faith Evans*	123
14	Man in the Mirror —*Michael Jackson*	135
15	Strength, Courage, and Wisdom —*India Arie*	143
16	Meant to Be —*TLC*	155
	Epilogue: Bruised but Not Broken —*Joss Stone*	167
	Acknowledgements	169
	Permissions	175
	Notes	177

Foreword

Life with suffering is inevitable. Not only will our physical bodies suffer but also we will face suffering from the result of sin, generational curses, worldly wickedness, and injustices inflicted by others. For some, suffering can birth a deeply rooted brokenness; but for others, it can birth an undeniable fire of faith and dependence solely on God.

When I first met the author of this book, I was in a broken season in my life. From our very first encounter, I sensed Torrie Chatman was a woman who has been through the fire but was able to see God's greater purpose through her pain. She carried herself with authentic strength, spoke with power, loved with grace, and encouraged others with deep understanding. To survive what Torrie has survived—God is the only possible reason for her incredible healing. What could have left her broken and bitter has instead given her strength to embrace her past and expose her scars as a canvas for others to learn from.

What you're about to read in these pages is less about Torrie and more about how we don't have to die in our brokenness because God's resurrecting power is all powerful. As you read this memoir, I pray her story ministers to you as it did to me. I pray you examine the areas in your life that are broken and seek the face of God for complete healing. I pray her revelations speak to your soul and drive you to repentance. She can teach all people that although you may be bruised, you don't have to be broken.

Ashley Joy
www.ashleyjoyspeaks.com

". . . we share our testimonies not so our lives can be picked apart but so someone doesn't have to face what we barely survived."

—Sarah Jakes

Introduction

Bruised but Not Broken was birthed within the depths of me long before I ever typed a word of it. I've personally been most affected by someone's message when they shared pieces about themselves because it let me know I wasn't alone. After imitating the messages that proved the most breakthrough for me, I felt God telling me to share my own pieces.

Music has also been instrumental in every aspect of my life, both helping me figure out what to do and soothing me during the toughest of times. Therefore, I named each chapter after a song that I felt sums up that chapter's theme.

This has been a hard, therapeutic, beautiful journey for me. My hope for you is that if you don't have something you desperately need, maybe you can borrow it from these pages. It may be strength, your voice, vulnerability, healing—anything you need so you can move forward. I pray this book inspires you. I may never meet you face to face, but know that my heart is with you.

CHAPTER ONE

This Woman's Work —Kate Bush

There wasn't a possibility of a TV show career or a lot of warm congratulations when my unwed seventeen-year-old mother, Michelle, started showing. She was an honor roll student anticipating her senior year of high school, and when she found out she was pregnant, she was ashamed and disappointed in herself. She really wanted to have an abortion, but she couldn't come up with the money.

But when I was born on December 1, 1983, all of that became a distant memory as the nurse placed me in her arms. The weight of the situation she'd found herself in was no match for the unrelenting love penetrating her soul for my seven-pound, ten-ounce body.

She wasn't the only one who fell hopelessly in love with the family's newest addition. My father, Darryl, was totally smitten with his baby girl. But co-parenting was difficult. Mama was kind and loyal and generous, but she also had a fiery and combative personality. Daddy, on the other hand, was calm and super laid back. They often bumped heads.

When I was about three, my mom and I moved to North Carolina to live with my great-aunt Diane and her husband, Stan. Diane thought getting out of our hometown, Wetumpka, Alabama, would be good for us. Daddy didn't want Mama to move so far away with me, but she made the leap anyway.

We weren't there long before Mama met my stepfather, Jack, and fell in love. Mama was the happiest she had ever been. She gained not only a life partner but also more family. Jack's mother, Granny, was a sweet woman who loved us as her own. And with Mama's infectious smile and Jack's outgoing personality, Mama made friends easily.

Soon Mama and Jack were expecting. I was almost five when Jessica was born, and I was so excited about being a big sister and having a live-in playmate. When Jessica got older and could sit up on her own, we'd go for walks after Mama got off work. She would pull Jessica in our red toy wagon and I would ride my tricycle alongside them. Mama was so happy with our family—for a while.

I don't know when Jack started hitting Mama or if I knew he was addicted to drugs while we were all living together. I do remember the yelling behind closed doors and Mama's face when she came out—eyes swollen and bruised, lips torn and bleeding. I remember Jessica wanting Mama to pick her up, but Mama couldn't because she was too sore.

This Woman's Work — Kate Bush

Once Mama told me to ask Jack to please stop hitting her. It took her a while to convince me; I didn't want him to whoop me for interfering in "grown folks' business." When I finally asked him, he roughly told me to go somewhere and sit down but didn't lay a finger on me.

On the outside, our family looked perfect. But the inside of our home became cold, unpredictable, and tense to the point that Mama became scared that Jessica and I would end up orphans. So Mama left Jack and took Jessica and me back to Alabama when I was seven, toward the end of my first grade year.

Moving back meant seeing cousins on a regular basis. I loved them all, but Ashley, my mom's sister's daughter, was my favorite. Ashley and I are less than five months apart and quickly became inseparable. Now, instead of taking interminable bus rides to see Ashley, we could be in each other's company within fifteen minutes.

Adjusting to being back came easily. We lived with my Grandma Betty as Mama recovered. Soon enough, we moved into our own house. Our weekends were filled with fish fries, jump rope, and hide and seek. We didn't always agree, but we were close family.

Upon returning to Wetumpka, I began spending a lot of time with my dad and his family. Daddy had gotten married and had two children with his wife. My brother DJ was three years younger than I and my sister Devan was five years younger. When I went to visit, Daddy was rarely around much. He and his brothers had formed a gospel singing group and they traveled most weekends, so

I spent a lot of time with his wife, DJ, and Devan. I loved my brother and sister dearly, but I never quite felt a part of Daddy's household. He took care of me financially, but our relationship was shallow at best. Conversation between us never went into depth. As much as I loved being with my brother, sister, and the slew of cousins Daddy's ten siblings had produced, I couldn't wait to be back with Mama.

Many changes had happened over the previous year, but more were to come. One of the best was Kristen. We were in the same second grade class together, and only one letter kept us from having the exact same last name: hers was Chapman. We were besties before the term was ever coined.

Besides having a good friend, I liked school and was a good student. My lessons were important to me, but one day I got sick during class and had to leave early. That day changed the rest of my life.

After my teacher called to let her know I was sick, Mama called around to see if someone could care for me so she wouldn't have to leave work. My great-aunt Diane had moved back to Wetumpka after Stan died, and Trey, her new boyfriend, offered to pick me. Trey seemed to be a hardworking family man. He helped Aunt Diane care for their children: the two my aunt had with her late husband, Stan, and the one she and Trey had together. But he must have seen his chance and jumped on it. It was the first and only time he had me completely alone.

When Trey picked me up, everything changed—not just for me but eventually for my entire family. On that day,

This Woman's Work —Kate Bush

he began molesting me. He showed me a porn movie and asked me to imitate with him what we watched. I knew something was wrong, but Trey knew I was an obedient child. If an adult told me to do something, I did it, even if I didn't want to.

Every other encounter between Trey and me was in a house full of people. He would catch my attention when no one was looking and signal for me to go to the back of the house, where no one else was. After he was done with me, I went back up front and did whatever my other cousins were doing. I pushed down whatever confusion I felt. I just blended back in and played with the other kids. I didn't want to do those things with Trey, but I didn't want to get into trouble.

From the moment he touched me, I became two people. I was an innocent, playful little girl with everyone else and someone and something I didn't understand at all with him. I was a girl dealing with an issue I should have never had to endure at the hands of someone my family trusted.

The molestation continued for about a year until the Saturday we were at Diane's house, preparing to surprise my great-grandparents with a party for their fiftieth wedding anniversary. Her house was buzzing with relatives, but Trey found a chance to motion me to the bathroom.

As he fondled my nine-year-old body, someone opened the bathroom door. Diane stood in the doorway, completely startled. But after staring for a few moments and taking it all in, she did what I hope few people would believe: she turned her back, closed the door behind her, and walked away as though she'd seen nothing.

Trey and I stood for a moment, both terrified. I just knew I was going to get the worst whooping ever. He was probably thinking, *I've been caught.*

After a few moments of stillness, he fixed my clothes and told me to go up front and play. I went to the front of the house as I was told and soon forgot about what had just happened. I did notice Diane was extra nice to me for the rest of the day.

Two days later, while I was in class, a message came in over the intercom. I was being checked out of school. Excited, I grabbed my backpack and raced to the office to see my mom's sister, Clockie, there to pick me up. My cousin Rhakevious was being checked out too. We played in the backseat and ate gummy snacks on the way to Diane's house.

When we got there, several relatives' cars were in the yard. I walked into the house, where most of my aunts sat with somber looks. My mom was sitting with them, tear stains streaking her face. Everyone's demeanor alarmed me, and I began to think someone had died.

Before I could sit down and figure out what was wrong, I noticed a police officer in the room. He said, "Hey, Torrie. How are you?"

"Fine," I responded in a cautious voice. Then he asked me what had happened to me that Saturday with Trey. I put my head down and began to cry. I didn't know if I was in trouble. I did know nothing would ever be the same again.

This Woman's Work — Kate Bush

From the moment the secret between Trey and me was no longer hidden, I felt dirty. Exposed. A doctor at the local hospital examined me. It seemed every adult I came into contact with asked me the same questions. I felt as if Mama woke up crying and went to bed crying every single day.

Another wave of emotions swept over my family a few days later, when Mama came home with cuts and bruises on her hands and arms. She kept saying, "She waited two whole days to tell me! Two days!" I didn't know who "she" was, nor did I ask. My focus was to stay as invisible as possible.

For some time after everyone found out about the molestation, Mama would call me into her room and question me. She repeatedly asked me for in-depth details of what had happened. Every time, I felt beyond ashamed. One particular day, she called me into her room and started asking me different questions. I sat there, sick with dread, as she asked me if Trey had threatened to hurt me if I told. In a tiny voice I answered, "No, ma'am."

Then she asked if he'd threatened to hurt her or my sister. She was really angry at this point and she screamed, "Why didn't you tell me?" Voice shaking, I told her I was scared. Then she said something I blocked out for almost twenty years: "You must have liked it."

I am amazed how our bodies are made to protect us, but still we're affected by pain. I blocked out those five words but digested them at the same time. I couldn't remember them until the day Mama told me what she'd said, but I operated in those words for almost two decades.

I did register what she yelled next: "Get out of my house!"

I was nine, barefoot, confused, and completely shattered. My innocence had been taken from me by a pedophile. The remaining fragments of my self-worth disappeared as the words left her mouth.

I stood. Tears gushed down my face as I walked out of the house. I stumbled across the yard but stopped once my feet hit the street. After figuring out which relatives lived closest, I decided where I was headed and began walking again. And as I walked, I cried. Each step solidified what the enemy wanted me to believe: what was happening was my fault, and I was alone.

I got a little more than halfway to the stop sign before Mama called me to come back home. She never forgave herself for what she said—and I never fully trusted her again.

CHAPTER TWO

M!ssunderstood —P!nk

I can still remember what Cedric and I were wearing my first day of seventh grade—the day he strolled back into my life. I was wearing the new school outfit I'd bought with Ashley when we'd spent our traditional summer week with our cousin Shan in Atlanta: a simple white top, Guess overalls with rainbow stitching, and Air Force 1 shoes. Cedric had on a black and white Hugo Boss shirt, jeans, and black tennis shoes while rocking the enormous picked-out afro everyone talked about. And those big brown eyes were the same ones I'd seen in the face of the boy I'd met years before.

We watched each other from a comfortable distance before slowly making our way to each other outside during a break. We smiled, greeted one another, and shared a brief hug. I uttered these words to him: "I noticed you noticing me, and I wanted to put you on notice that I noticed you too, and I might consider letting you be with me." Who remembers *The Fresh Prince of Bel Air*? My words flowed smoothly with a slight bit of cockiness.

Cedric put his head back and laughed, and I joined in. That was our beginning.

He was beyond popular with the ladies. Among his flavor of the week over at our school, he had an on again/off again girlfriend named Allisen. Benkie was her nickname. For the first half of that year, Benkie and I had a serious rivalry over this knuckleheaded boy. Whether it was trading insults over the phone or me thinking I was big and bad by approaching her bus while students departed for the day, we never passed up an opportunity to get at each other verbally. I didn't spare Cedric an assortment of words either, even when I technically had a boyfriend. I just couldn't shake Cedric.

When I was in junior high, being in a relationship meant you met at football games and shared Sour Patch straws and held hands in the hallways. Cedric and I never quite got there; we talked over the phone and saw each other at school. During one of our good days, we slid off in the gym. Cedric pulled me in and gave me my first kiss. Between the puppy love I was developing for Cedric and my infatuation with R&B music, I felt inspired and began writing poetry.

Soon enough, my interaction with Cedric fizzled and life went on. The passion I developed for writing deepened as I fell more in love with lyrics and Mama constantly slipped books in my hands so I wouldn't watch TV during all of my spare time.

Mama introduced me to books when I was around ten, and from that moment, I was hooked. Instead of getting toys or candy for good grades, I got an R. L. Stine book instead. I was enamored that in a matter of minutes, I could see life through someone else's eyes and be in a different place altogether.

Along with my love for books, I got my passion for music from Mama. She was into all kinds of music, but anything sung by Tupac Shakur was her favorite. Among our musical roster were Master P, LL Cool J, Monica, Brandy, Aaliyah, anyone in the Bad Boy Family, and Xscape. Sunday's music was my favorite, though. While a lot of my friends spent the Sabbath in church, the Chatman/McClamb household spent the morning cleaning to Marvin Gaye, Al Green, Mary J. Blige, and TLC.

Despite my refuge in books and music, being a teenager could be just plain hard. From seventh grade to tenth grade, I was constantly fighting with other girls for one reason or another. I remember sitting in the principal's office after a few altercations, not even knowing why we'd gone to blows in the first place. When we were asked how the fight started, often the other girl said, "She thinks she's cute," "I heard she likes my boyfriend," "She thinks she's better than everybody," or "I just don't like her." Rumors were usually the cause of all the confusion and friction.

Honestly, I absolutely hated fighting, but I defended myself no matter what. You want to fight? Cool. I tried to get the other girl to throw the first blow, but if she'd been picking on me for a while, spreading lies and subtly bumping into me in the hallway, I'd allow my emotions to take over and swing first.

My weapons of choice were Mama's nursing school books, which she sent to school with me if I told her I'd been having problems with someone. "Just bust 'em in the head with it!" she'd say. And Ashley, of course, wasn't going to let anything unfair happen. She fought side by side with me several times—and then did in-school suspension a few cubicles over from me. I won some, lost some, and flat out fought the air once as the other girl and I barely touched each other while we swung.

We were all fighting some invisible battle that had nothing to do with what was in front of us. Mine was insecurity. While all the other girls were developing curves overnight, I felt as if my body were stuck in elementary school. The jokes about my flat chest, nonexistent behind, and skinny legs bothered me to the core, to the point that I began stuffing my bra. That stopped one day in the lunchroom when a classmate told me to look down. The tissue I had carefully molded into a believable size that morning had found its way out of my bra and was now poking out of my shirt. Never again! I couldn't risk having "Torrie stuffs her bra" circulate in whispers for days until something else grabbed the student body's attention.

The insecurity and altercations just made me shrink more into myself. Many of my classmates saw me as a snob, but really it came down to one simple thing: I did not trust people. Just about every aspect of my life had proved I shouldn't. So I cut off everybody except my tiny circle of friends—Ashley and Kristen, of course, and Freddy and Alicia, two other close friends—and carefully decided what I could share with them.

As I transitioned into high school and had classes with students of all grades, I began to loosen up a bit and allowed more of my personality to show. I did well in school, but not as well as I could have if I'd applied myself more. Nevertheless, I managed to maintain a B average. Throughout my high school career, I was in JROTC, poetry club, the girls' varsity basketball team, dance team, and the gospel choir; I also managed to hold down a job. I purchased my first car on my own, a blue Ford Escort, and paid my own phone bill and insurance. I took pride in having my own responsibilities.

CHAPTER THREE

Fallin' —Alicia Keys

It had been years since Cedric and I were an item, but we were friendly whenever we happened to meet. I dated and fell in and out of what was love for me, and he did the same.

After running an errand one July afternoon, for some reason I drove a little farther up the road and ended up at Cedric's place. We caught up and sparks flew. I had no expectation of what was to come. All I knew was that for the rest of summer break, I looked forward to seeing him. By the time school started in August, we were officially a couple.

Cedric was what the homies and I considered one of the bad boys, and all of us seemed to be going through a phase with Wetumpka's finest. Cedric had dropped out of high school and had a local job. My friends and I had just started our senior year. The year's goal was to kick it, have fun, and roll right out of our small hometown when graduation was over.

I was enamored with Cedric. He seemed to have more insight about life and had experienced more than the guys at school. I never intended for us to get serious, but I couldn't deny the butterflies that spread from my heart to my lips whenever I saw him. Suddenly all the rainbows and sunshine we were experiencing together came crashing down when Hannah showed up at his house.

Hannah was his ex-girlfriend—and the mother of his daughter, Chasity. Hannah had gotten word that Cedric and I were a couple, and she was not happy about it at all. She hadn't allowed Cedric to see Chasity in months because of their disagreements. Now he was eager to try to get along with Hannah. I knew the game Hannah was playing, so I was ticked, but I wasn't going to make him choose between his daughter and me. My heart ached for a real relationship with my own dad. I didn't want Chasity to know what that felt like, but her mother made it very hard. Hannah was a white girl, and she said every obscenity she could to me without directly calling me the *n* word.

There would be nights when she would sit in her car in Cedric's yard, blowing the horn until he came out to talk to her. She told me once that my mama, grandmamma, and I needed to go back to the field and pick cotton. In the same breath Hannah had the audacity to tell me to have my own monkey so I'd have someone to put in the backseat of my car. Since she'd clearly forgotten that Chasity was biracial, I reminded her of her own part "monkey" child. I knew

Fallin'—Alicia Keys

Hannah was all talk and no action, but I made it very clear to her that if I ever caught her outside the safety of her car, I would come after her.

This foolishness went on for a solid month until she realized she wasn't going to scare me away, and she disappeared. Cedric could see I was getting tired of all the drama. In the midst of all of this, I'd allowed my relationship with him to consume my world. I saw him every day, even if it was for ten minutes. I stayed at his house when he wasn't there. My friends and I barely hung out anymore outside of school, but they had their own things going on too.

Beyond the baby mama drama, the first sign I should have paid attention to came the evening we were hanging out at his place and a new video game he wanted had come out. He asked me to buy it for him and I let him know I didn't have enough money. I can't remember verbatim what Cedric said, but his words cut deep. My breath escaped me because I was so stunned. All I wanted was for us to be happy, so I told him I could pay part of the money. Cedric jumped up out of his seat so we could go to Walmart to purchase the game. After leaving the store with his new game in tow, I admitted that he'd hurt my feelings. He apologized but was so excited about this game. I took what I felt and tucked those emotions deep inside. I had no idea they would soon violently erupt.

Things went on smoothly for a few months. It was my senior year, and I was thinking about my next step. Since I was nine years old, I'd dreamed of attending Clark Atlanta University, as one of my older cousins had. But

Cedric's and my budding love and our talks of our futures together—and the cost to attend Clark—persuaded me to weigh my options. The University of Alabama, Faulkner University, and Stillman College were the in-state schools I was considering. I'd taken the ACT several times since my junior year; my highest score was a 22. I decided anywhere I was going to go had to take that score.

Another option was snagging my attention as well: the United States Army. I loved JROTC and was currently the JROTC Cadet Lieutenant Colonial of Elmore County. After talking with my teachers and Cedric, the Army became the top contender. If Cedric and I were really going to have a future together, this was a great step in my mind. I could go to school for free through the G.I. Bill.

2002 seemed to roll in so swiftly. I approached Cedric one evening early in January and told him I was getting ready to graduate and needed to know what my next move would be. We'd discussed marriage a bit, but part of me didn't think he was going to go for it. Basically, I told him either we needed to make plans to get married or I was going to college in Atlanta after graduation.

The next day, he got down on one knee with a ring we'd casually viewed from time to time at the local Walmart and asked me to be his wife. In my Captain D's uniform, with tears streaming from my eyes, I said yes. At school the following morning, I sat Kristen and Kisha down and told them I was marrying my bad boy. I think more than anything, they were relieved I wasn't pregnant. An engagement could be called off; a baby, not so much.

Fallin' — Alicia Keys

My girls were the easy ones to break the news to. My mama, on the other hand, urged me not get married so young. I assured her that we were happy and in love and didn't want to be without one another.

Cedric and I decided to get married soon after graduation, so I let my JROTC teacher know I needed a recruiter. After setting everything up, I went to the headquarters in Montgomery to take a test to see what jobs I was qualified for and what my leave date would be. I decided to become a Telecommunications Operation Maintainer, and my leave date was scheduled for July 22, 2002. I would do basic training at Fort Leonard Wood, Missouri, and advanced individual training (AIT) at Fort Gordon, Georgia.

I was thrilled and frightened all at the same time. I was eighteen, but I was still a kid. I'd never lived away from my mama. We bumped heads a lot, but she was all I had. Instead of confiding in her, I put on a brave face. The interaction between us was at its worst. I was rarely home to see her. When I wasn't at school, I was working. If I wasn't working, I was with Cedric. Mama had heard some things around town about him. I attempted to assure her that his baby mama was crazy (she was), but not everything Hannah was saying was a lie. Yes, I'd heard Cedric talked crazy to her and had hit her, but I ignored the rumors. I'd only experienced his mouth. He was cutthroat, ruthless, and downright heartless when he got mad and didn't get his way. But that was minor and could be fixed, right? The love we had was enough to conquer the world. I wanted and needed to believe that.

CHAPTER FOUR

Love is Blind —*Eve*

Spring break was approaching and I wanted to spend unlimited time with Cedric. So I told Mama I was going Panama City with some of my friends, as I had done for several years. She was fine with it. I had a girlfriend pick me up from home and take me to Cedric's. He and I stayed up late, talking and watching movies, and I stayed in his room while he was at work.

Everything was great until that Sunday. We got into an argument that went further than our normal yelling and cursing. This time he hit me, and I fought back—hard. I pulled his hair, kicked him, bit, screamed, and scratched any piece of his skin I could get ahold of. He wasn't much bigger than I was, but I was no match for his physical makeup. He mostly hit me on the top of my head because he knew his blows there wouldn't leave marks.

Kristen was set to pick me up at the local store around five, so Cedric took me to meet her. The car ride was quiet and awkward. I felt as if the air were being sucked out of me. I couldn't believe what had happened and just wanted to get away from Cedric. As Kristen drove away, she fussed about me being done with him, and I covered up the scratches on my face and neck with her concealer.

Once I was finally satisfied with how I looked, Kristen dropped me off at me off at my aunt's house, where my entire family met to eat that evening. Everyone asked how Florida was as my mom looked at me strangely; she knew something was off but couldn't tell exactly what.

As I ate with my family, I didn't want to be there. I hated what Cedric had done to me, but I was torn because I still wanted to be with him. I was also distracted with worry that the makeup didn't conceal all of my wounds. I should have been more concerned with the hidden blemishes that ran much deeper.

It didn't take long for Cedric to start calling my phone, and I found some excuse to slip away to go home. But instead of going home to gather my thoughts, I went straight to my boyfriend, who'd beaten me up hours prior.

Soon Mama started calling, but I didn't answer. I should have known she would just show up at Cedric's. Before things could get too heated with her and everyone in walking distance could hear, I left his house and drove away while Mama called me every name she could think of.

As she followed right behind me, Mama flashed her headlights several times, so I pulled my car over. Mama jumped out of her car, walked up to my door, and yelled for me to let my window down. As soon as the window was down far enough, she reached back and punched my ear as hard as she could. For a few moments, everything went white. Before she could hit me again, I pressed my foot all the way to the floorboard and pulled off.

I drove over ninety miles an hour to try to beat her home to grab my toothbrush and a change of clothes. Before I could make it to our front door, I heard her car rounding the corner. I wasn't willing to take any more hits from her, so I got back into my car and pulled back out of the driveway.

She yelled after me, "Get out of the car, Torrie!" All I could do was cry and shake my head.

Finally, I took off down the road, too frightened to look back. I called Cedric, told him what had happened, and asked him to come meet me somewhere to pick me up so I didn't have to wander that night. We decided to hide my car in a parking lot behind a local nursing home.

This night changed everything. I'm not saying I was right in being disobedient to my mom. But here I was, with both of these people saying they love me, yet both of them hitting me. I was beyond tired of being Mama's punching bag in more ways than one. She barely laid her hands on me anymore, but I had received more verbal and mental abuse on a regular basis than I cared to remember. Cedric promised never to hit me again, and more than anything, I wanted that to be true. I needed it to be true.

Which was the right one to choose, and why did they have to be the choices? No one should have to choose between an abusive lover and an abusive mother. I picked

Cedric and lived with that decision for the next year and a half.

I lived with Cedric and his parents for the next two months as his girlfriend. On May 31, I became his wife. I wore a simple slip dress. Cedric bought a red collar shirt, but I had to ask his mom to get him to tuck the shirt in.

When we arrived at the courthouse, Mama put a bouquet in my hand. She made sure I had something new, something borrowed, and something blue. Since she'd realized there was no way I would change my mind, she figured being apart from me was better than being ostracized from me; she'd found out the hard way that I would pick Cedric over everything.

Abihail and Alicia were the only friends in attendance, along with our immediate family. Daddy held my hand and walked me down the aisle to Cedric.

I didn't have a relationship with God, but I knew what Cedric and I were doing was serious. I stared into Cedric's brown eyes and got lost in the hope of our vows. He promised to love all of me and I did the same. I threw all of our issues out of my mind and focused on the beauty of our moment.

The ceremony seemed to go by in an instant. We'd scraped up enough money to hire a photographer, who took pictures as I smiled and giggled and my new husband whispered in my ear. I'd willingly signed on for a lifetime with Cedric, but I didn't really have a clue what I'd gotten myself into.

About a week before my leave date, my mom and I scrambled to get everything I needed for basic training. The night before I was shipped off, the military put Cedric and me in a hotel room. We'd been married less than two months, and I was getting ready to leave for five months for basic training and AIT.

I lay awake on my hotel bed, contemplating changing my mind. But what would our next step be? I hadn't turned in a college application because Cedric had asked me to marry him. He hadn't graduated from high school. We were newlyweds living with his parents, anticipating being able to establish ourselves through the military. I'd gotten security clearance for my job. We would have housing, insurance, and so much more covered. This was the best choice for my family. I wiped the tears out of my eyes as Cedric talked about our future together. He was sick about me leaving.

The next morning, Cedric, Mama, Jessica, and Grandma Betty joined me as I finished processing to leave for my basic training at Fort Leonard Wood, Missouri. Aside from my being sworn in, we spent the day waiting, watching TV, and talking. Finally, it was time for me to leave. I had never flown before, so I was terrified. After our tearful goodbyes, I boarded the plane. Everyone on the small charter flight was going to basic training.

It was very early morning when we arrived on base. The Army processed us quickly so that they could put us in the barracks. I cried the hardest that first night. It was my first time being away without anyone I knew.

After being on base three days, we finally got our things and were able to change. By then, we'd been given our camouflage battle dress uniforms (BDUs) and were allowed to call home to let our families know we'd made it safely. I cried the whole forty-five seconds I was on the phone with Cedric.

Before we could go to our squad, we had to take a pre-physical training test that consisted of three categories: push-ups, sit-ups, and a timed two-mile run. I was barely 110 pounds, but I was out of shape. I couldn't do the mandatory three push-ups and failed the test. This failure added two extra weeks to my stay in Missouri. I was devastated, but those two weeks ended up being such a blessing. I had to go to the remedial unit, or "fat camp," as the soldiers called it. I toned up quickly and prepared to take my PT test again to enter basic.

Every day in basic training was an adventure. We were taught hand-to-hand battle tactics, how to shoot a rifle, and so much more. Although I woke up tired and went to bed exhausted, I gradually found my way. I stuck to myself for the first few weeks, but eventually I became really good friends with a beautiful Latina named Amanda. Being completely out of my comfort zone, I began to see what I was truly made of.

I received packages from Mama every week, along with cards and encouraging letters. Cedric wrote me just about every day. When I got further along in training,

I could talk with him on the phone more. I found out Hannah was allowing him to see Chasity on a regular basis and Mama had even spent some time with her. Things seemed to be falling into place.

What I loved most about the military was that it enabled me to take care of myself. I was in the best shape of my life and becoming more confident each day. As basic training was coming to a close, my mind shifted to AIT at Fort Gordon. I was looking forward to learning my job while being closer to home.

After I'd been away for over three months, it was finally time to graduate. Almost everyone I wanted to show up did, except my dad and his family. A few days before leaving for basic training, I'd sat down and had my first open and honest conversation with him. I told him that although I was an adult and a wife, I needed him. He promised to make more of an effort to build a relationship with me.

I received maybe two letters from him while I was in training. As soon as I found out my graduation date, I wrote him, hoping he would come. When he wrote back and said he and his family couldn't make it, I mentally wrote him out of my life again. I was tired of being disappointed by him and decided it was better to go on as I had been without him.

So I graduated, and the rest of my family looked on with pride. The moment our drill sergeants released us to go to our families and I laid eyes on Mama from across the parking lot, we both took off running toward one another.

To this day, it's the most memorable embrace I've ever experienced. Her embrace melted every fear inside me.

I was able to spend the afternoon with my family as we caught up. Grandma Betty, Clockie's family, my mama's brother Cody, and Cedric all made the journey to be there for me on that day.

Within twenty-four hours, I was back on a plane, this time headed back to the South. Once we got to Fort Gordon, we were told we could have a weekend pass. After driving seventeen hours, Mama and Cedric drove another four hours to come get me. It was great being back with my family and my husband. We went to the movies and saw family as I indulged in all of my favorite foods. On Sunday, I returned back to AIT and began to count down to the end of this part of my military journey.

In AIT, we continued to have PT at dawn, but what we were eating was no longer monitored. Although I wasn't fat, I wasn't in shape the way I'd been in Missouri. That revelation came out two days before Thanksgiving, when I failed to do the minimum sit-ups required to go home for the break. At first, I was devastated, but then I realized I could sneak out of my window early that morning and be back before bed check that night. So that's what I did. Cedric called me at 4:00 that morning when he made it on base, and by 8:00 a.m. we were in Wetumpka. I'd never missed a Thanksgiving with my mama and wasn't about to this year either.

My last weekend at Fort Gordon, some of the girls in my barracks and I decided to get tattoos. I'd been contemplating getting a tattoo of my husband's name. He had several tattoos, and I wanted to prove to him that I was committed to our marriage. I called him and asked, "Babe, do you really love me?"

His response: "Of course."

"And we're going to be together forever, right?"

"Chatman, I ain't going nowhere."

That was all I needed to hear to make my mind up. A couple of hours later, I got my husband's name tattooed in the small of my back. When he showed up to visit me the next day, he was elated. We jumped right in the car and headed to the same shop so he could get my name tatted on his back.

When my mama came up the next day to help me pack to go home, we showed her our tattoos. As she laughed until she cried, she said, "You two dummies! Y'all are both stupid!"

Cedric and I didn't care. We laughed along with her. The tattoos solidified our bond, and nothing was going to come between us. Crazy, bruised, immature, whatever—I was his and he was mine. That's all that mattered.

CHAPTER FIVE

Nobody Knows —*P!nk*

After I graduated from AIT, I got to go home for three weeks for Christmas. The three "f's" consumed my time at home: family, friends, and food. Needless to say, I was in heaven.

During this time, ironically enough, I forged a beautiful friendship with one of Cedric's exes, Benkie. She was pregnant with her and her husband's first baby and lived next door to Cedric's family. Who would have thought the same girl whose neck I wanted to ring all those years ago would be so supportive of all my endeavors?

On Christmas Day, Cedric called Hannah and asked her when he could come over to give their daughter her gifts. Hannah replied that she didn't want him to come anywhere near Chasity. She refused to bring her over or allow him to stop by. Right before the phone call ended, Hannah told Cedric that I needed to try to have a baby with my uncle.

That was one of the few times I'd seen him cry. We were getting ready to move to New York and he had no idea when he'd see his child again. I consoled him while my own scars stung. It seemed that no matter how many years had passed, I could never outrun what had happened to me as a child. Clinging to each other, we decided that soon we'd start trying to have our own baby.

Unfortunately, that phone call wasn't our last encounter with Hannah while I was home. Several days later, we pulled up at a convenience store while she was walking out. After a good ten minutes of arguing back and forth, she told us Chasity wasn't my husband's baby. That was her usual statement whenever she got ticked at Cedric. Chasity had several of my husband's features, so I figured Hannah was lying as usual. But if she wanted to play that game, I'd go there with her.

I'd been dealing with her for a year and a half, and I was sick of her antics. I told her we weren't going to beg her for a child and since Chasity wasn't Cedric's, there was no reason for her to ever contact us again. I told her she needed to lose our numbers and forget where my in-laws lived and, basically, she could get into her car and drive off the face of the earth. The fact that Cedric had married me, fused with the things he'd done while they were a couple, pushed Hannah to agree with me. I gave her the biggest farewell coupled with some insults, and then we left. That was hardly the last time we heard from her.

In the meantime, I went back to my high school with some Army recruiters for a week and saw my old teachers.

When I was asked how I liked the military, I hardly had a good response to give. Frankly, it wasn't what I'd expected. I still hadn't adjusted and, although I didn't know it at the time, I was battling depression. My orders had arrived several weeks before, and I was not pleased. My duty base was at Fort Drum, New York. It was located at the very top of the state. We were going to be eight hours away from New York City, two hours from Syracuse, and thirty minutes from Canada. Anyone who knew where Fort Drum was located always asked, "Who did you tick off?" I also knew Fort Drum had a high deployment rate, and I did not want to be shipped out. But this was the path I'd chosen, so I had no other choice but to comply.

I did love the fact that Cedric and I were thriving and our relationship was better than ever. The time apart did wonders in our marriage. Plus, I'd been able to purchase a brand new car. I was pleased with every area of my life except my career choice.

Before I left, the military sent the movers to come pack up all our belongings and shipped them to New York. My family gave us a going away dinner. On the morning we left, we lingered in the embraces of his parents and my mama. We got into my car and I waved through the back window until I could no longer see Mama's face. I then turned around and grabbed Cedric's hand as we started this new journey in our life together.

As we drove up the coast and the hours passed by, we marveled at how the weather went from seventy degrees in Alabama to snow. There were moments I reached over and wiped the tears from my husband's eyes and he did the same for me, but our tears were short-lived. The buzz of excitement about our lives outweighed the uncertainty of leaving everything we'd ever known. After driving over twelve hours, we stopped in Maryland to spend the night. Maryland was the shortest state for us to drive through; Pennsylvania was the longest.

As we pulled up to the base, we both perked up to see the place we'd call home until I was stationed somewhere else. I couldn't believe my eyes. Soldiers were all over, doing evening PT in negative fifty-three-degree weather. Most of them literally had icicles on their noses. Immediately, I knew I wasn't going to make it there for long.

After checking in to let my platoon know I'd arrived, Cedric and I checked into a hotel. We called that place home for about a week before we got word that we had military housing. Both of us were happy to settle into our new town and have a home-cooked meal.

During processing, we were given a questionnaire that asked how we felt, what we thought, and how we'd been coping with military life. A couple of weeks later, I was contacted about going to counseling.

Even if I didn't cry every day, I just felt down. And Cedric felt the brunt of my emotions. We'd been doing well for the most part, with no major arguments since a month before I'd left for basic training. We purchased furniture and other necessities for our new apartment. We'd even gotten a new puppy we named Dakota.

Depression, unspoken fears, insecurity, and plain boredom were bound to come to a head. And they did the day after Valentine's Day. While I was in basic training, Hannah had started allowing Cedric to see Chasity. Around the time I was graduating from basic training, their senseless arguments had started back up, so Cedric had started seeing Chasity less. Apparently, Cedric recorded some video during my time in basic when he spent time with Chasity. We'd set up boundaries that he wasn't supposed to go past Hannah's living room, but one of the tapes showed him deep in Hannah's house.

I was beyond livid. Both Cedric and Hannah were notorious liars and the last thing I wanted was for him to give her the opportunity to create a story plot. In the video, he was in Hannah's bathroom while she was giving Chasity a bath. What sent me into a frenzy was the fact that Hannah's hair was wet. To me, that meant she'd probably just gotten out of the shower when Cedric arrived and he was in the back of her house while she was half dressed.

I came out of our bedroom screaming and calling him every name imaginable. Why would he do that? Was he not thinking of us while engaging in bath time with his daughter and crazy baby mama?

The verbal argument turned into one of the worst physical altercations we'd ever had. We fought off and on from about 2:00 p.m. to 9:00 p.m. until I locked myself in our second bedroom. Cedric took my phone and a change of clothes and left.

When he didn't come back the next day, I walked to the store, got a prepaid card, and asked a neighbor to use her phone. I called several times, and between my continuous sobs and pleading, he let me know he was in Connecticut with some of his mother's family.

The next day, I had to call in to work because we lived thirteen miles from the base and Cedric still hadn't come home. I rented a car and got a loaner phone so I could have some kind of communication. Then I filed a police report on him. He'd hit me first and I'd defended myself. I'd scratched his arms up with a knife. But the bruises on my skin had nothing on the ones in my heart, in my mind, and on my self-esteem.

When the police told me they couldn't make Cedric bring my car back, I told them the car was mine and he wasn't a joint owner. The police called him and told him he had twenty-four hours to get the car back to me. As long as he wasn't in the state, there was nothing they could do. The police got the title information faxed to them only to discover that the car was in both of our names. I'd thought the car was in my name only and Cedric had only signed as a cosigner. That wasn't the only issue I had on my hands. Because of our altercation, I lost the logistics and security clearance I needed for my job.

Later that night, Cedric came home and we made up. At that time, the military took domestic violence very seriously. I was forced to move into the barracks and told not to have any contact with him. I spent one night in the barracks and went back home the next day.

Since I'd lost my clearance, I was moved upstairs to my commander's office. Because of everything that had happened and my inability to adapt, I was offered the option of going to the reserves or getting out altogether. I opted for the latter. My commander began the paperwork for me to discharge and I couldn't have been happier.

After being in my position for a few weeks in the commander's office, I started getting random emails from a particular address. I knew the culprit was Hannah. I started calling her house day and night but never got an answer. Finally, one evening her dad answered and stated that Hannah wasn't home. When I asked when she would be back, he said May. Well, it was March.

At that point, I used the skills I'd learned in AIT. I was able to take the IP address and track Hannah all the way down to the house in California where she'd sent the email and the phone number of that house. I waited until my break to call since New York is three hours ahead of California.

"Hello, may I speak to Hannah?"

"Just a moment."

"Hello . . . "

"I told you to leave me and my husband alone. You said the baby wasn't his, yet you keep appearing. I heard you'll be back in Wetumpka in May. Guess what? Me too, and I'll be back to regulate. When I see you, I don't care if you are holding your baby or walking with Jesus Christ Himself; I'm gonna get you." I hung up in her face.

When I got home that evening, I found out Hannah had been calling Cedric and lying about her involvement with the emails all day long. I was over it and had made up my mind. I'd kept silent and made idle threats long enough, and my lack of real action had made her bold. I decided that when I saw her again, my threats would be idle no longer.

Meanwhile, Cedric and I were halfway getting along. Then we got into another fight, and instead of traveling two states over as he'd done during the last blowup, he went all the way home to Alabama. Per our usual cycle, he came back home and we made up and went back into our honeymoon phase.

At the beginning of May, my orders came for me to be discharged on May 22. I was ecstatic. I could not wait to get home to my family, especially my mom. A week before I left, Cedric and I stayed in a hotel while our apartment was cleaned out. We'd become *American Idol* fans, and I'll never forget that the night before we left New York, Ruben Studdard, a talented man from Birmingham, Alabama, won. We cheered in our hotel room.

This was one of the periods when I fell truly in love with music. P!nk stole my heart during the VH1 show *Beyond the Music*. So did Alicia Keys, Jennifer Lopez, and TLC with their *Fan Mail* album. P!nk's song "Nobody Knows" spoke volumes about where I was in my life.

But no matter how hard I tried, I couldn't shake the darkness surrounding my life. Cedric wasn't to blame for everything. There were moments he truly attempted to be selfless and understanding. He ordered a spiritual book from a commercial he saw on TV and even started praying for our marriage. Because of all we'd experienced and my own demons, I didn't acknowledge his effort.

When we drove away from New York, I felt relief. This chapter was closed. Finally, I would be home with my family and maybe Cedric and I could grow and be better together. Maybe . . .

CHAPTER SIX

Ex-Factor — *Lauryn Hill*

Everyone was excited that we were back. We spent the first week visiting family and looking for jobs. Cedric followed some prospects while I landed a job as a server at Ruby Tuesday.

On our way to my mom's house two weeks after being back, we passed by the local library and I spotted Hannah's car. Two years of pent-up anger and frustration boiled over. After we walked into the library, I sat directly across from her at a computer. When she noticed me and then saw Cedric, who'd wandered into the kids' room to see Chasity, Hannah grabbed her things and darted to Chasity.

What happened? I ended up spending two hours in jail for fighting her. In the moment, it was worth it.

Looking back, what was I doing with myself? I tried to cave in her face with my fist, but for what?

I should have told Cedric to keep me from fighting her, but he, of course, was down for whatever. We were both frustrated with the ins and outs of dealing with her: talking, debating, and silence. We'd tried to compromise with her and get rid of her, but nothing worked. I figured if she knew I wasn't playing with her about causing her bodily harm, then she would stay in her lane. This was a terrible approach, but ironically enough, I never had to fight or argue with her again.

On our first anniversary, May 31, Cedric and I exchanged simple gifts. We smiled, laughed, and held one another. We thought that since we'd made it a year, we would ultimately be okay. Neither of us had any idea our marriage wouldn't make it another three months.

When Cedric got a job, we were on different shifts most days. He worked 2:00 p.m. –10:00 p.m., and I worked whenever I was needed to try to make ends meet. We began fighting again, worse than before. The first physical altercation after we got back caused me to move back home with my mama. I filed charges on Cedric but later dropped them. We were building quite a reputation with the police station.

I think what made him madder than anything else was that I always fought him back. The fights all started the same: raging tempers and careless words. We hit below the belt, destroying one another's self-esteem, our love, and ultimately each other's bodies. Nothing was off limits.

I remember staring into the mirror at one point and not being able to recognize my face. Who was this person staring back at me? As tears welled up in my eyes, I touched every part of me that was physically hurting. I started at the knot on my forehead and allowed my tears to spill over as I touched the ring around my eye. The deepest cry inside me was screaming, *How he could do this to me?*

It would be years before I realized we weren't swinging at each other but at ourselves. Our self-hatred was destructive. We were like F3 tornadoes, destroying everything in our paths. One day we were in love, the next day in hate. People say it's a thin line between love and hate. That line was surely on its way to becoming invisible.

A month after I fought Hannah in the library, Cedric and I saw her late one night about to exit Walmart as we pulled up. In moments we were out of the car and walking toward her. Once she spotted us, she didn't continue to walk toward her car or retreat back into the store. Instead, she grabbed Chasity by the hand, walked quickly to the kiddie pools, and, picking one up, pretended to look at it. When we reached them, Cedric immediately knelt down and started talking to Chasity. I said, "Hey, Hannah."

She pretended to be absorbed in the sturdiness of the plastic in her hands. I knew she was using it as a barrier to keep me from hitting her, but I knew better. There were too many cameras and possible witnesses to even go there with her, and anyway, my plan was spook her more than anything. I greeted her again a little louder.

"Hey, Torrie," she responded. I looked over and saw Cedric playing with Chasity, who he hadn't spent any time with in over six months, so I made small talk with Hannah. Once she understood she wasn't in any danger, she put the pool down. Cedric saw the opportunity and asked Hannah if he could see Chasity soon.

I have no idea what possessed her to say this, but she invited us to her house the next day to talk and spend some time with Chasity. Cedric and I were skeptical because Hannah had no problem calling the police and I still had to appear in court in a few weeks because of our incident at the library. She promised she was sincere. We agreed to go over but didn't decide until the next day to go for sure.

For the first time ever, we conversed like adults, hashed out our differences, and focused on trying to create some stability in our interactions for Chasity's sake. The plan was that Cedric and Hannah would figure out what worked best with visitation and Cedric would support Chasity financially. Cedric agreed to let me know all interactions with Hannah.

Our living arrangement at this time was a little different from that of most married couples. If we were in love, we stayed with his parents. If we were cordial but I didn't know if we'd argue, we stayed at my mama's. If we were in dislike or hate, we stayed separately. The night before everything came crashing down, we were at odds, and I had spent the night at Mama's place alone.

When the mailman came that morning, I received a bill, along with login information to set up accounts online for our newly purchased phones. I followed the instructions and set up accounts for us both. Once I got through the basics, I looked at his call history and was furious to see he'd made some calls to Hannah I'd known nothing about.

I immediately called Cedric and cursed him out. Instead of admitting I'd set up an account online, I told him the bill I'd just received documented even the calls between him and Hannah from the day before. Before he could peel off a list of excuses, I hung up.

I called Benkie crying and admitted to her that no matter what, Cedric wouldn't do right. Benkie, nine months pregnant, was on her way to a doctor's appointment; but between my sobs, she told her husband, Tony, to turn the car around. I told her not to and settled down. She promised to call me once they were done in Montgomery.

Every time Cedric called for the next hour, I hung up. Then he popped up at my mama's house. The look in his eyes let me know instantly that he was ready to put his hands on me. Before he could, I dialed 911 and let it ring once before hanging up. Then I picked up the biggest vase in my sight, dashed it across his head, and started swinging at him. Sadly enough, I'd learned how to fight my husband. If I stunned him by hitting him hard with something first, he wouldn't beat me so badly. I was sick of being the only one with visible war wounds. I fought until I had no breath left. By then, the police had arrived.

Neither Mama nor Jessica was home, and I knew the altercation could last a while if someone didn't intervene. That's why I called the police. They had to respond to calls even if the caller hung up, so I knew they would be there within five to seven minutes. I knew if I could hang on until then, I'd be fine.

Our next fight was the first and only fight that landed us both with a twelve hour stay in the local jail. I had a lot of time to think while I was in that cell.

Mama was constantly begging me to leave him. For a few weeks, my family and I had been secretly discussing me moving to Atlanta to start over. Fighting had gotten beyond old. It seemed as soon as our bruises healed, we covered them with new ones. It was only a matter of time before Cedric's actions pushed me to do what I didn't think I would have the strength to do.

But how could I walk away? Escaping to Atlanta sounded good, but I didn't know if I truly had the heart to do it. I felt stuck. I didn't want my marriage to fail. Cedric had been embedded in my heart for seven years. He was my partner in crime, and although what we had was turbulent, each of us would handle anyone who came against the other. He was the strongest and most consistent example of "love" from a man I'd ever experienced. Yes, we fought and destroyed one another with our words, but he never fully walked away. Daddy would disappear for months over a disagreement, but Cedric never did. He would convince me to talk to him and we'd end up making promises we couldn't keep. Not because we didn't want to. In my heart

Ex-Factor —Lauryn Hill

of hearts, I believe we genuinely wanted to be better for one another but didn't know how to. So no matter what happened that day—whether the police had been called or we both had black eyes and bruises racking our bodies—my heart found solace as I listened to his heartbeat.

After I was discharged, I promised myself I'd never spend another minute in jail; so when an argument started to escalate, I'd simmer all the way down. Our arrest, which had taken place at a local convenience store, was our town's current gossip. I was beyond embarrassed and was trying to convince Cedric we needed to get ourselves together and move fifteen miles away to Montgomery. He felt we didn't have anything to be ashamed of: to him, our affairs were no one else's business.

We didn't stay overnight with each other much because tension was high with our families. We were sharing the car to get each other back and forth to work, but our relationship had definitely shifted.

When Cedric dropped the car off to me at work one Saturday night, we had a minor disagreement. His brother had trailed him to my job, so Cedric left as quickly as he'd come.

We'd gotten into this groove of not contacting each other for two days after a disagreement. But instead of waiting until Monday, I showed up at his job when his shift began the next day. A coworker told me Cedric had called in claiming to have a meeting with the family lawyer.

I left and drove straight to his house. He wasn't home and his dad hadn't seen him all day. I then drove to his mama's job to see if her car was there. It was, so Cedric wasn't using it.

At that realization, I was truly puzzled. Where was he? I had no way of calling him because I'd thrown his phone up against a brick wall the previous month for talking to Hannah without my knowledge. Cedric was a loner and only had two friends. A phone call to one and a visit to the other proved him MIA.

I drove back to his house and checked again to see if he'd come home. Still no Cedric. I went back out to my car, let my windows down to catch a breeze in the summer heat, and waited next couple of hours for him to show up.

While I waited, I prayed. I cried and had honest dialogue with a God I hadn't acknowledged or talked to in a long time. I asked Him to show me if Cedric was being unfaithful because I didn't want to have children with that kind of man.

Around 9:30 p.m., I drove to his mom's job because I figured she'd probably pick him up from wherever he was after she got off at 10:00. She drove straight to the house as I trailed her from a distance. When she got out of the car, I asked her if she'd seen Cedric. She said she hadn't heard from him but would ask his dad. In thirty minutes, I was gone; his dad hadn't heard from him either.

Drained and hungry, I drove to a store not too far away from the house. Cedric's brother, Jeff, was there on the pay phone. I stood there, waiting for him to finish talking, and then asked where Cedric was. Of course, Jeff said he didn't know. Jeff explained, "I'm headed to Montgomery to pick up my girlfriend from work," but I didn't believe him. Since he was the last person I'd seen Cedric with, I felt sure Jeff was going to pick him up.

We said our goodbyes and I let Jeff get on the highway before I pulled out to follow him. The entire time I was behind his car, I asked God to reveal what I needed to see. About five minutes away from Jeff's girlfriend's job, I realized he actually was going to pick up her up. Something told me to turn my car around and head back, so I did.

The previous week, Benkie had told me she'd seen Cedric out in our yard talking to a girl in a red Acura with a 3A license plate tag. When I'd questioned him about it, he'd said some relatives had come into town and other relatives who lived in Montgomery brought them to visit in their car. I said okay and didn't think anything else of it.

When the light from the local diner brightened the street five miles away from his house, I realized what kind of car I was behind: a red Acura with a 3A tag, the same car Benkie had told me about days before. I could see Cedric's head in the passenger seat and a woman's head in the driver's.

Then I knew. I knew she wasn't a relative but, instead, the other woman. My heart dropped and rage surged through my body. I turned my lights on bright and drove as close to the car's bumper as I could without hitting it.

Instead of driving to his house, the mystery woman and Cedric drove to his grandmother's home. I think a couple of things were going through Cedric's mind. He needed more time to prepare this girl for me, and he thought I wouldn't cut up too badly at a relative's house.

He was telling himself lies. I didn't care at all about where we were.

As we came to a stop, the rapid beating in my heart echoed in my ears. Was this really happening? After grabbing a solid wooden miniature bat I kept in the backseat, I got out and walked up to the driver's side of the Acura. The stranger in the driver's seat had fixed her eyes straight ahead. I stared at her until I could no longer take being ignored. I tapped her window with my bat and asked her who she was.

As she mustered up a weak "his cousin Lisa," he jumped out of the car. "Stop acting crazy! She's my cousin."

Ignoring Cedric, I asked her, "Who are your parents? Why have I never heard of you before?" After she basically whispered her responses, I asked her to let her window down because I couldn't hear her.

Cedric came around to my side of the car and tried to get me back into my own car. In the calmest voice I could muster, I said to her, "We both know you aren't his cousin, and since I don't know what he told you, I'll go ahead and set the record straight. I'm not his baby mama, his girlfriend, or some girl he deals with on the weekend. I'm his wife. I have his last name. And if I ever catch you near my husband again, I'll slit your throat."

Her face reflected exactly what I wanted it to: fear and shock. Grabbing a bag from the back seat, Cedric said we needed to go home and talk. I hit him a couple of times with my bat and asked him to explain the change of clothes.

Ex-Factor — Lauryn Hill

He started to give me some lie about her doing his hair and I cut him off.

When we got into the car, I told him, "Before we go home, we are going to where 'cousin Lisa' lives."

He then exited my car and got back in with her. I trailed them to his parents' house and jotted down Lisa's tag number. When they pulled into the yard, I blocked them in and blew my horn. I'd barely put my car in park before I jumped out.

Hearing my horn, Cedric's mom came out of the house. I asked her if Lisa was her niece. She shrugged and said, "Sure." It was so apparent she was lying.

I went back and forth between arguing with him and questioning Lisa for the next hour. Finally, Lisa blurted out, "I didn't know he was married."

I looked at his hand and his ring was on. I swung at him. I don't know whether he'd slipped it on while he was in the car with her or whether he'd worn it while he was doing God knows what with her. Either way, the betrayal cut deep as my mood went from one extreme to the other. I reiterated to Lisa that if I caught her remotely close to Cedric ever again, she'd regret it for the rest of her life.

Tired of the useless back and forth, I drove my car out of the yard and pulled onto the street. Whenever Lisa decided to leave, I was going to follow her. After a few minutes, Cedric walked up to my car. Between cussing him out, I told him I planned to follow Lisa home. He lunged through the window and snatched my keys out of the ignition. When they fumbled out of his hand and hit the floor, he grabbed me, yelled for Lisa to leave and get far enough ahead that I couldn't find her, and held me down for twenty minutes. I tried with everything in me to shake his grip, but he was stronger.

When he let go of me, I grabbed my keys off of the floor and drove home to my mama's. By then, it was close to 2:00 a.m. I went into the house and collapsed next to Mama's bed, tearfully telling her Cedric was cheating on me. Mama lay there and let me tell her everything as I sobbed. She didn't hug me or offer me words of comfort. She just said, "What are you trying to do? Save him from the next woman that he'll beat and cheat on? Let him go, Torrie."

For years, I was mad at her response. After peeling my body and broken heart off her floor, I left, got into my bed, and cried myself to sleep.

The next morning, before she went to work, Mama came in and wiped my hair off my forehead and kissed my cheek. It took me a long time to understand why she waited until then to comfort me. She'd witnessed firsthand how destructive Cedric's and my relationship was and knew it wasn't going to get any better. She'd watched the same young woman take her first steps, held me while I teethed, and watched me go off to kindergarten. Here I was, an adult but still her child. I was going down a road she knew all too well. I was now her nineteen-year-old child, being abused and misused by a man who said he loved me. So she knew speaking honestly and bluntly in that moment was best for me.

Ex-Factor —Lauryn Hill

The next afternoon, I packed everything I owned in my car and moved to Atlanta. I called early that morning and had my job transferred to the Buckhead location. Mama advised me not to tell Cedric that I relocated, so I didn't.

Some may wonder why I opted to move. I knew if I stayed, I wouldn't have been strong enough to stay away from Cedric. Our cycle would have continued: I would have ended up right back in his arms—and he would have ended up right back in my heart.

CHAPTER SEVEN

Don't You Forget It —*Glenn Lewis*

Atlanta was definitely a culture change, but there wasn't a part of the city I didn't love when I encountered it. The city was rich in countless cultures, and the people seemed to be working vigorously for the tomorrow they envisioned for themselves. This pace was completely different from the easygoing, more settled atmosphere in Wetumpka.

Moving to Atlanta gave me the push to want more for myself and more out of life. My days were busy juggling two jobs, so I usually went home and collapsed after my shift. But on the nights sleep didn't come easily, I missed my husband.

Cedric called every couple of days from a payphone to tell me he'd find me eventually. I'd advised everyone who knew where I was not to tell him, but after each call, I questioned my decision to move. Weeks later, when my cousin spotted him in a local club with two women, I was finally confident I'd made the right choice.

That decision was further confirmed when Kristen told me Cedric had been sleeping with one of our classmates while I was in basic training. However, instead of using my head, I allowed my emotions to get the best of me and drove back to Wetumpka in the middle of the night to confront him. We argued for hours but didn't lay a finger on one another. I knew it was time to for me to do everything possible to move on with my life.

Someone told me I could possibly get assistance through Legal Aid and divorce him for nearly nothing. I called and set up an appointment back home as soon as possible. The next time I got on the road to head down 85 South, it wouldn't be to confront my estranged husband; it would be to start the journey of ending our marriage.

Due to our résumé with the local police station, I was able to get my divorce process started at no cost. Once the paperwork was in order, our local sheriff attempted to serve Cedric at his house twice before his dad accepted the paperwork. When his dad gave him the papers, he called me, and the outrage I heard from the other end of the phone was simultaneously comical and annoying. Cedric's rants ranged from "My parents are so upset about this paperwork!" to "What kind of wife leaves her husband and moves out of state?" You would have thought I was the one who cheated on him. That was just the first of many calls during our divorce process.

Meanwhile, I began the journey of finding out who Torrie was. I wore colored contacts, embraced my skinny legs, and began writing poetry again. I dated a little, hung out with my coworkers, and became mesmerized with my roommate Shelly's Jamaican roots. I can't pinpoint exactly when I finally realized I would be okay, but after a while, I didn't have to fake a sense of happiness or peace.

Early one week in October, Kristen invited me to homecoming at the University of Alabama, where she attended college. I didn't have much left after I paid bills, so I told her I couldn't afford to come. She told me that if I got there, she would take care of everything.

That weekend in Tuscaloosa changed everything for me. For the past few months, I'd planned to live in Atlanta for a year so that I could be deemed a resident. That way, when I picked a college, tuition would be cheaper. But then Tuscaloosa showed me a great time. For only a few days, I got to act my age.

A week later, Kristen suggested that instead of waiting to go to school in Georgia, I should attend UA. She went to student services and got me an application. When I came back for Halloween, I filled out the paperwork and had her turn it in for me. In less than two weeks, I received my acceptance letter for fall 2004. My heart was set on starting school in January 2004, so I made some calls and secured my status as a freshman for the spring.

I was so excited to tell my family I was about to attend the best school in the world. Before I knew it, Thanksgiving had arrived. I decided to move back home over the holiday and finish out the year in Wetumpka rather than Atlanta. I transferred my serving job back home. Once Kristen completed the school semester, she came back.

Everyone we'd hung out with in high school was back on Christmas break, and we all had a great time.

One night, we ended up at the same club as Cedric. I should have known we would bump into each other eventually. A quick glance in the mirror behind the bar confirmed I still looked cute. At some point, he made his way over to me. We made small talk and parted ways shortly, but I knew his eyes were on me for the rest of the night. As soon as the club shut down, he asked me to go somewhere to talk with him. Cedric pulled the car around, and I sat in the passenger seat.

I'd been drinking, so it took me a few moments to realize we were in Lisa's car. The instant the memory clicked, I tried to get out of the car. I realized either the door was broken or the child lock had been activated.

Having trapped me in the car, Cedric began lying to my face again about his real relationship with Lisa. It didn't take long for me to begin to panic at the thought of what could happen if we did get into a full blowout. I hadn't fought him in almost five months, and I liked my face looking normal. To my relief, he got out of the driver's seat, walked around the car, and opened my door.

I got into the car with Kristen and headed home. We were both drunk. This was the first of many nights I look back on and know it was the grace of God that got us home safely.

Before I knew it, it was 2004. I was at my grandmother's house getting ready to travel to Tuscaloosa to start my new venture. I was stoked.

Before I left, Mama pulled me into her chest, wrapped her arms around me, kissed me on the cheek, and said, "I'm so proud of you, baby!" That meant everything to me. For the duration of my relationship with Cedric, I'd felt I'd continuously disappointed my mama. Now her smile and words permeated my heart.

When we got to Kristen's apartment a few hours later, we lugged my stuff inside. She'd offered to let me stay with her that semester and we agreed to find somewhere bigger for the summer.

The next day, Kristen and I woke up early, got dressed, and headed to campus so she could show me the basics before heading off to her own classes. My first stop was financial aid. I got my ACT card (my school ID card, which could have money put on it) and then headed over to the Ferguson Center to purchase my books. I wandered upstairs and somehow ended up in a Starbucks line for the first time. The barista had mercy on me despite the long line and didn't correct me as I mispronounced the names of the beverages. I'd unknowingly stumbled into an addiction for lattes with whipped cream. As I headed to my first class, I was nervous and excited but knew I would feel at home in no time.

By the end of the day, I'd gotten lost on the huge campus, dropped my books, and slid into my classes right before they started. But I was absolutely thrilled. It was crazy to think that months before, I was distraught, lost, and brokenhearted. I finally had some type of much-needed direction.

After the first few weeks, I got into the groove of my five classes and started working as a server at a local restaurant. After two weeks there, I met Jordan. He was tall and cute and had a contagious personality that drew everyone around him. A junior at a nearby college, he was in a fraternity and maintained good grades. It didn't take long for me to set my eyes on him. However, there was a slight problem: he had a girlfriend.

As awful as it sounds, my mindset was "out of sight, out of mind." It all started out harmless. He invited me to get-togethers at the house he shared with his roommates. Then he started confiding in me about some issues in his relationship, and I did the same about a guy from back home I'd recently started dating.

As we worked together one day, he ended up telling me his plans after graduating college, which included marrying his girlfriend, Erin.

I was a little flabbergasted. "So you're going to marry her, even with all you've told me about the relationship?"

He said, "It doesn't make sense to break up with her. She hasn't done anything wrong. In fact, she's a good girl. I'm not completely happy with her, but that's the next step after I get settled into a job as a music teacher at a high school somewhere."

"But you're going to marry her out of obligation because you've been together most of college? That doesn't make any sense."

He shrugged it off and we moved on from the subject. We still ate together after work, shared jokes, stole glances, and gave endless compliments; he still invited me to stay after the bulk of his friends had gone home. I knew how to play my hand. I took a mental note of everything he liked and disliked and the current events in his life.

It didn't take too long for Jordan to break up with Erin and turn his attention on me. I had no idea I shouldn't have been entertaining any guys since I was still technically married. No one talked about healing or the fact that I was an adulterer too. I was just having fun with the carefree life I'd skipped to become a wife.

CHAPTER EIGHT

You Gotta Be —*Des'ree*

My carefree attitude got me an A and a D my first semester. I only got two grades because halfway through the semester, I dropped my three other classes. Everything had my focus but school. Jordan was smart and worked hard in class, so I tried to follow his example during summer school; eventually, though, I fell back into old habits.

After June, I became roommates with Kristen and two girls she'd met during her freshman year, Amber and Christina. No one told me having four young, opinionated women under one roof would be disastrous. I really wanted my friends to like Jordan because I'd gotten so much backlash about Cedric, but they didn't.

In the midst of my relationship with Jordan, I befriended his friend Kayla. Through Amber's sister, Angel, who attended the same college as Jordan, my roommates and

I found out about a rumor that Jordan and Kayla were more than just friends. I didn't believe it, but my roommates didn't care for either of them and subtly let them know whenever one of them stopped by our place.

My roommates and I were also bumping heads about a cleaning schedule. A divide was definitely occurring, but no one addressed it outright at first. After a few months, I dreaded being home and found any excuse not to be there. I was looking forward to our lease ending so that I could move out the following year.

Although my relationship with my roommates wasn't the best, my relationship with my mom had gotten significantly better. I guess the saying "two grown women can't be under the same roof" rang true for us. We talked several times a day about everything and nothing. Sometimes all in the same day, we laughed, argued, missed each other, and got tired of each other. For the first time ever, I began to see my mom as my friend.

But my dad and I still only talked about surface stuff: "How are you? What are you doing? How are x, y, and z?" While I was home one summer weekend, I suggested we go out to eat. It wasn't completely awkward, but it wasn't comfortable either. It had been years since we'd been alone together.

I struggled to ask Daddy for anything, but being a college student and working was creating a strain on me. My brother DJ had just stared college that semester and his needs topped mine every time. I felt very much like an afterthought in my father's world.

Most of the time, I avoided asking him for anything because it seemed he could never come through for me. I'd work when I needed to be studying and mention it to Mama, and then she would work more to help. Eventually, she caught on to me avoiding asking Daddy for anything and asked me why it was so hard for me to turn to him. Between the tears, I told her he wasn't reliable and simply did not care. She called him on three-way and finally understood what I dealt with whenever I tried to communicate a need to Daddy.

My desire was for an active, involved parent. Was it because I didn't grow up in his house or experienced too much so soon? Most encounters with Daddy and his family reminded me I didn't belong. But no matter what, I could always count on Mama. She was all in if I was wrong and all in if I was right. No matter what we endured, even if I felt misunderstood, I knew she wanted me.

Although my home life wasn't completely peachy, my social life was buzzing. I was making friends and learning the ropes around UA. During my history class that summer, I met Chrishauna. She was sassy and ridiculously smart. I loved how she never sugarcoated anything. Parties were still going strong, so I was still kicking it with my new friends. I figured since I wasn't taking such a heavy load, I could be lenient on myself and just study here and there. Besides, I'd never had to study in high school. And it was the summer!

Before the term was up, I ended up on academic probation. I had to plead my case so that I could keep my financial aid and stay in school. I had no way to pay for it myself, nor did Mama. She helped as much as possible by buying groceries and books and getting my car repaired when necessary. Finally, right before fall, my aid was cleared so that I could attend the upcoming semester.

I geared myself up to get ready for my first football season at UA. I was more intrigued by the atmosphere that the time of year ushered in than by the games themselves. The semester started off as usual with the Greeks heavily on the scene. I looked for any sign of the sorority Delta Sigma Theta. Most of the girls I'd begun to hang out with had been on campus longer than I had or knew more about the organization than I did, so they told me everything about the sorority. My heart was set on pledging the next time the Deltas had a line. I knew I had a lot of work to do to get my grades up, so I began getting things in order.

Jordan's senior year started off well too. He was a drum major and president of his fraternity. I was consumed with everything concerning him. I fixed my work schedule so that I could be off during his home games. After the games, if Jordan's fraternity was hosting a party, I was in attendance. I was present at way more activities at his college than I was at UA.

In the middle of that semester, I decided I wanted to major in theater. I was taking some thought- provoking classes and meeting some of the most talented people I'd ever encountered in my life. These students knew what they wanted and owned their roles and the stage whenever they stepped on it. I truly adored theater, and my English class didn't rank that far behind it. My teacher, Jan, was a petite, freckle-faced, redheaded woman who made me fall in love with words and reading all over again. I genuinely looked forward to her class and the assignments we received. English homework didn't seem like work at all.

One day after class, Jan asked if I'd declared my major and minor. I told her I was probably going to major in theater. She suggested I think about making creative writing my minor. I told her I would definitely consider it. I treasured the acknowledgement that I was good at something because I hadn't done so well in my classes up until this point.

Other than that, my life revolved around Jordan. I settled into the role of being his right-hand man. We laughed and carried on like nuts with each other. We were coworkers, homies, and lovers. We genuinely enjoyed one another's company, but when it came down to it, neither of us was whole. We'd each never healed from previous relationships. Instead of taking time out to deal with ourselves individually, we disguised underlying issues with each other.

I was always wondering if I measured up to his ex-girlfriend, Erin, though I never said it to anyone. I'd heard she was a smart, sweet girl. Everyone who knew her loved her. And since both Jordan and Erin were majoring in music, they saw one another every day. That was enough for me to play the comparison game in my head for a while.

Since Jordan was so active at school, I figured it would only be a matter of time before I bumped into Erin. At a party during early spring semester, we formally introduced ourselves. I instantly understood why she was spoken of so highly. I knew if our circumstances were different, we'd probably be really good friends. After that, whenever we saw one another, we'd always hug and make small talk.

In mid-March, I closed the book of Cedric and me for good with the finalization of our divorce. When we were summoned to a hearing the second time, he actually showed up. We hashed out who would get what, and then the judge signed the paperwork. I was officially a free woman. I'd never been so excited to write a check.

My theater classes hadn't lost their zeal, so I decided to officially declare theater as my major. I began to dig within, press past my feelings, and apply myself in my studies. Before I knew it, I was attending Jordan's graduation that May. He'd worked so hard, and I was proud of all he'd accomplished. I'd registered for the extensive summer semester along with the first summer term, but before that started, Jordan and I went on a vacation to the Bahamas as his graduation gift. Between his graduation and our departure, we didn't have much time to rest, so we were exhausted most of our vacation. Nevertheless, we enjoyed one another's company.

The environment with my roommates was evolving for the better. In December, things had come to a head with the growing tension and a bunch of "he said, she said" stuff. We were pleasant with each other for the sake of living together, but then Amber and Angel's father passed away on Mother's Day, and Kristen, who'd left at the end of the fall semester, gave birth to her son. After a birth and a death, we decided to squash all previous issues with one another.

After our vacation, Jordan went home to visit and decided to move back to Montgomery. I was sad but had been mentally preparing for him to find work elsewhere. I was home in the living room eating when my roommate Christina came in and said she'd just seen Jordan in the mall with some of his friends. I found it weird that he hadn't told me he was in town. I called him, and he said he'd just gotten there a while ago and was just about to call me.

A warning went off in my head. I then asked him if he wanted to kick it that night, but he told me he'd already planned to hang out with his friends. We hadn't seen each other in while, so I was eager to spend some time with him. I suggested that we link up after he and his friends did whatever, but Jordan insisted we could hang out the following night. In my gut, I knew something was wrong, but I didn't give off any hints of my suspicions.

After our call ended, I thought for a few minutes before walking across the hallway to a friend's apartment. I told her I was cheating on Jordan and the guy's apartment was close to some of Jordan's homeboys. Then I asked her if I could borrow her car because mine could possibly be spotted. My friend agreed and I told her I'd be back later to get her keys.

Although Jordan had moved back to his hometown, his things were still in the apartment he and his roommate, Brian, shared. My plan was to drive by around midnight to check things out. Until I got ready to leave, I quieted myself but kept my hands busy. What was I about to discover?

I got ready, got my friend's keys, and headed to Jordan's old apartment. To make sure I passed by exactly when I felt I should, I drove slower. The way his apartment was positioned, I had to look back over my right shoulder to see his front door. Jordan's car was there and so was his roommate's. Nothing looked out of the norm.

I continued driving and then turned around. As I passed by to exit, I breathed a sigh of relief. I softly chuckled at my paranoia, but to make sure I could scold my instincts, I turned around and drove past his apartment one more time.

My dismissal of my gut feeling came about two minutes too soon. As I passed by and glanced back, I saw Jordan and Erin walking up the stairs to his apartment.

I didn't think before I swung the car around. I pulled up on them so fast that they barely had time to turn fully around. I rolled down the window and said their names with the most venom I could muster. "Hey, Jordan. Hey, Erin!"

I was gratified by the stunned looks on their faces. Erin walked quickly into the apartment. I got out of the car and followed them both up the stairs. Erin disappeared into Jordan's room, and he and I went into the kitchen, where we talked for the next forty-five minutes.

Jordan offered me excuse after excuse: "She's leaving for Chicago tomorrow for grad school. I love you. No, I've never cheated on you with her."

My mama had this saying: "The same way that you get them is the same way that you lose them." Did I not know this guy had a girlfriend when I met him yet knowingly dismissed this other woman's feelings toward him? I absolutely did. Erin probably cried more tears than I could count because of my actions. Now it was my turn; I was reaping what I had sown. While pursuing instant gratification, I wronged Erin and shortchanged myself.

Before leaving, I stepped into Jordan's room and told Erin to be safe on her way to Chicago. A confused look crossed her face, but she said thanks. On the way to my car, I made a mental note of the car I figured she'd driven over since I knew she didn't have one.

Would you believe this was just the beginning of our night? After Jordan didn't answer when I called him an hour later, I drove back to his apartment in another friend's car and, of course, the car Erin had borrowed was still there. At that point, I went back home to get my own car.

By the time I returned to his place at 3:00 a.m., I was beyond livid. I had just caught him with his ex a couple of hours before and she was still there? Naw. I wasn't having it.

The pain of betrayal took a backseat to the rage rising up in my chest. After knocking on the front door with no answer, I walked around the building and started yelling his name up at his window. When I went back to his front door and he finally answered, I asked if she was still there. Jordan replied yes.

I used every ounce of strength to try to get past him to Erin, but I couldn't. So I started swinging as hard as I could at him. With every punch, my heart shattered a little more. I'd done everything to show him how much I loved him, but once again my best wasn't good enough.

With all of this drama, it made perfect sense to just cut my losses and walk away. I didn't. I continued to focus on how much I'd invested into our relationship. My logic outweighed the idea that maybe Jordan wasn't the one for me.

My discovery at the beginning of the summer was nothing compared to my discovery at the end of the summer. In my heart, I'd known Erin and Jordan's late night rendezvous wasn't an isolated incident, and the emails I read when I figured out his password confirmed it. The two of them had been sleeping together most of the spring semester. I was devastated. I was being cordial with this female because Jordan had to see her every day on campus and she was everywhere he was outside of class. And I was still buying into the hype that our relationship was worth fighting for.

Why was I undermining one of the most valuable parts of my existence: my heart? I had yet to come into the knowledge of Whose I was, so my issues kept controlling me and hurting others.

CHAPTER NINE

Imagine Me — *Kirk Franklin*

From this joker I was hoping would make me his wifey in the future down to my daddy, I had man issues and I knew it. Although I had problems, I also had friends to help me take my mind off my worries. And what do college kids do when they have struggles? They kick it!

I was indulging in the norm but was slowly becoming curious about God. My friend Holly helped immensely. We were introduced to each other by a mutual friend and when she started to attend Bama in the fall, we instantly clicked.

One of the most captivating qualities about Holly was her faith. If she believed something, it happened. She was always talking about God and quoting scripture. Holly made me gospel CDs and was always repeating what her grandma said about Jesus.

We attended football games and parties together and fed each other on a regular basis. Holly was always dragging me to some athletic game or some part of campus I'd never been to before because I'd been so busy running behind Jordan. What really solidified our bond was that she had man issues too.

One night, while Holly, a couple of friends, and I were in the cafeteria eating, I ran into Kobie, a guy I'd modeled with in high school at a local mall back home. I guess I was in my feelings about how things were unfolding in my world, so I confided in him about my relationship, or lack thereof, with my dad. Kobie listened attentively and exposed me to another viewpoint of my situation. He called me strong and said God was keeping me. He also told me my perseverance reminded him of the song "Imagine Me" by Kirk Franklin. As soon as I got home that night, I found the song on the internet and instantly fell in love with it.

Even though I didn't think I was as strong as Kobie said, I felt good after talking to him and receiving his beautiful encouragement. I had no idea of everything that would come from our short reunion over overpriced cafeteria food.

Not long after, I was leaving dinner with some friends when I received a call from my dad. Our last conversation had been six months before, when he'd refused to help me get a loan for summer school. My logic figured something was wrong, so when I answered, I skipped a greeting altogether. "What's wrong? Is it DJ or Devan?"

"Huh?" he replied.

"Are you hurt? Who's sick?"

Imagine Me — Kirk Franklin

"No, I'm not. Everyone's fine."

"Well, what do you want?"

Silence. Then, "Well, I saw your mom in the grocery store tonight and I decided to call."

"So if you hadn't seen my mom, then you wouldn't be on my phone?" I didn't let him answer the question before I started my rant.

As long as I could remember, Daddy had never invested into me emotionally. He never knew my favorite color, my favorite food, or my best subject. He didn't know what made me laugh. So here he was, probably genuinely concerned, but I tore into him with my claws out. I was tired—tired of feeling unwanted and burdensome, tired of paying for the mistakes between him and Mama. She was a handful, but I never had to wonder about her loyalty to me or my position in her life. She let Jessica and me know every chance she got that we were her biggest accomplishments. With Daddy, I just felt like a burden.

It was spring 2006, my junior year, and I was becoming a seasoned student by this time. I'd finally found balance in my academic and social lives to the point where neither suffered. I changed my major to telecommunications and made theater my minor. Audio and video production had caught my eye through some electives I'd taken, and I felt it would be a better career choice.

I'd attempted to pledge Delta and ended up not being picked for the intake process. Out of the nearly two hundred ladies who'd attended rush, forty-three were picked. Several of the girls who made the line had become acquaintances, so I was thrilled for them but sad for me.

Instead of staying in Tuscaloosa during summer break, I went back home. My cousin Ashley had given birth to a baby girl she'd named Summer, so I wanted to spend some time with them. I got a job at an electronic bingo hall, and when I wasn't working, I was spending time with family. It was refreshing to go home to and wake up in the same house as my mama. She used to tell Jessica and me that she rested best when both her kids were safe under her roof. Mama and I would go to the casino, indulge in our favorite foods, and shop. Home definitely had my heart.

The absolute highlight of break came toward the end of July. I was headed to work early one morning, driving along and listening to a gospel CD I'd made. "Imagine Me" began to play, and I sang along with the melody, but this time was different from all the other times I'd listened to it. This time, I felt something unfamiliar awakening inside of me.

This song is dedicated to people like me,
Those that struggle with insecurities, acceptance,
and even self-esteem.
You've never felt good enough
You've never felt pretty enough.
But imagine God whispering in your ear,
Letting you know that everything that happens
now is gone.

Imagine Me —Kirk Franklin

As the song continued and mentioned everything from depression to scars disappearing, I lost it. I didn't know what true freedom looked like or even how to start the journey to get there, but I did believe that just maybe I could experience it. What I couldn't say with my lips, I confessed in my heart. In that moment, I accepted Jesus as my Savior.

I called Mama and told her what happened, and she said in a warm tone, "Why are you crying? This is a happy occasion and one of the best decisions that you could have ever made." I was still so moved by what just happened that I couldn't answer. Little did I know I had just experienced my rebirth.

Two weeks after I gave my life to Christ, I got baptized. Since Jessica had never been baptized either, she did as well. The situation with Jordan was up and down already, and things between us took a nose dive when he neither showed up to my baptism nor even bothered to call. When I did hear from him, he used the excuse that he was working in retail in Atlanta and couldn't get off.

I was slowly reaching my breaking point. I went weeks without contacting him and avoided his calls. Jordan showed up on my doorstep at 3:00 a.m. the weekend school started for the fall. I did my best to keep my heart distant, but I allowed myself to get sucked into the *what ifs*. We had been together, as dysfunctional as we were, for two years. That's a long time in the college world. As much as I wanted to stay mad, I couldn't. I wanted him to know the changes I was making in terms of my new walk with Christ, and I wanted him. Plain and simple.

He was supportive of my transformation until it came to celibacy. When he left to return to Atlanta, he didn't bother to pick up the phone to call me. When I called him, he would answer, claim to be busy, and say he'd call me back, but he never did. I did what I knew I had to do: unfriend him on Facebook and go home to talk to my mama. While explaining the situation to her, I admitted I felt if Daddy had been around growing up, I wouldn't have experienced half the things I had when it came to men. He would have told—and, more importantly, shown—me how I was supposed to be treated.

Mama's response was, "Why do you feel like you want your dad so much?" At the end of any day, Mama was all I had. She was nowhere near perfect, but she did everything she could for us to have a good life. You see, I needed her, but I wanted him, and that she couldn't understand. The deep longing for his presence didn't discount all Mama had been to me. Even with all his flaws, no matter how many times I declared I was done with Daddy, I wasn't. This pattern went beyond my father and me. It leaked into every relationship I had. Wanting to be loved recklessly and fully consumed me, and when that desire wasn't reciprocated, a part of my heart was closed off.

Jordan's and my relationship came to an abrupt, nasty end months later. I hated that it was such a bad ending, but I was relieved it was finally over.

CHAPTER TEN

Golden —*Jill Scott*

It took me around a month, but I shook off the funk from my breakup and welcomed the solitude. I read more, laughed more, and breathed so much more easily. I discovered we are so terrified to lose what we've built in our own minds, but when we allow things and situations to fall away, we experience peace. I attended summer school, lost twenty pounds, and traveled somewhere random with my girlfriends just about every weekend.

Finally, the summer came to an end, and I prepared my mind and heart for my last semester at Bama. Right before classes started, a classmate invited me to attend Daystar Family Church. This is when my relationship with Christ began to take shape. When I'd started my walk with Him a year before, I was very legalistic in the *do*s and *don't*s of Christianity. I desired to have what the gospel I listened to talked about, but I had no idea how to fall in love with Jesus. Daystar showed me. By no means am I saying a one-eighty occurred, but I was taking baby steps. Church became something I looked forward to. I loved that I got to worship with people of different ethnicities and got to come as I was. I'm not just talking about wearing jeans to church. I finally felt safe enough to take my troubles to God. The atmosphere was life-changing.

Football season in Tuscaloosa is magical. Everywhere you go, there's a sea of crimson. Yelling "Roll Tide" excites any establishment. I made sure to take easy classes so I could spend time doing whatever I wanted. And it's a good thing I did because I attended rush again and was selected with forty-five other girls to go through the intake process to become a member of Delta Sigma Theta. Not only did I gain the women I went through the process with but also I entered into a worldwide, lifelong sisterhood with women from every continent all over the world! And we crossed on my birthday. It was the best birthday I'd ever had.

Before I knew it, graduation day came with all its emotion and beauty. The weather was in the mid-seventies, and I honestly felt God smiling down on me. I was amazed as I reminisced on all I'd achieved in those four years in college.

When I arrived at Mama's hotel room early Saturday morning before the ceremony, I couldn't even greet her before I started crying. She wrapped me in her arms and held me. The University of Alabama wasn't just my accomplishment; it was hers as well. It was where she'd planned to attend before she got pregnant with me.

Golden —Jill Scott

The day was about more than just me being recognized for receiving a degree; a dream was fulfilled, and the possibilities of a future were endless. Every family member and friend who'd encouraged and supported me beamed with pride. This was our victory.

Right after my graduation ceremony, my sorors circled around me and the other graduates in our organization to serenade us. I had no idea what my next step was, but I chose to live in the sweet moment in front of me. After the "Sweetheart Song" was over, my great-aunt Kathy pulled me aside and reminded me of the words she'd spoken to me over five years before. Right before I'd graduated from high school, she'd told me the Army wasn't for me and I should rethink my plans. Kathy grabbed my hand and said, "See, I told you you were a college girl!" For the first time that day, I didn't care what my face looked like as the tears fell.

After graduating, I worked retail jobs and endured one hectic summer term of graduate school. Graduate school sent me straight into the arms of God. Pastor Scott often told us God had incredible plans for our lives, and I wanted to see it with my own eyes. I was tired of being lost, so I pressed. Every Sunday, I was at the altar asking for prayer to get through the next week of grad school. I would have been embarrassed, but my need for strength pushed me to a posture of prayer. I stretched myself academically and spiritually, but my economics classes showed me that continuing my education wasn't for me.

Just eight months after graduation, I landed my first big girl job at Enterprise Rent-A-Car. My new job allowed me to pay my own bills and offered health insurance and 401K options.

All of that was great, but the best thing I got from ERAC was a new friend, a young lady named Jenn. She taught me everything she knew about the company. I'd never met anyone like her before: her outside completely matched her heart. She'd graduated from Bama and had a great fashion sense. Her vocabulary was impeccable; she taught me a new word every week.

2008 had brought a new job and fresh revelation of God. Then, just weeks into 2009, my dad called and told me my grandfather's health had drastically deteriorated. I packed a few things in my overnight bag and traveled to my hometown.

My grandparents' house was packed with my father, his family, his ten siblings, and their families. My dad and two of his siblings lived next to each other on the same road as my grandparents; everyone stayed in one of their houses. Two other siblings lived around the corner. At that time, there were thirty-three grandchildren and eleven great-grandchildren. It was a heavy time for us as a family, but there ain't nothing like food, smiling tots, hugs, and the retelling of stories to uplift your spirits.

A few days later, my grandfather passed away. His death caused a switch to flip on in Daddy. The days of pleasantries quickly vanished, and the foundation I'd wanted for years began to form between us. He held onto me a few more seconds when we embraced, and phone calls from him started to become the norm. I was grateful for the relationship I doubted I would ever experience. The insecurity of my existence being a burden began to heal.

As I spent more time with Daddy, I began to see how similar we were in so many ways. We would both throw our heads back when we were tickled. We shared the same nose and tried to see the good in everything and everyone.

Though my relationship with Daddy was better than ever, my attempts at relationships with other males weren't going so well. Dating was trying, and I wanted more. I was twenty-five; I had a decent job and was getting that itch to settle down. I'd never been great at juggling guys. "Serial monogamist" was an accurate description of me. I would start out conversing with three guys, and within three weeks, I'd be down to one.

Right before my grandfather died, I'd participated in Daystar's yearly twenty-one days of fasting. I made a bold declaration throughout the fast: I was going to get married soon. I didn't lie.

I'd met Walter on MySpace and we'd inboxed each other for a year and a half. When we finally went on our first date, my first instinct was to never see him again. The entire three hours were so awkward that I told Mama he was a word not even worth mentioning and declared I was never going out with him again. But he kept calling, and for some reason I kept answering. A month into us dating, I called him out on trying to care for people from his head and not from his heart. He took what I said seriously, and he seemed to transform right before my eyes.

Overall, Walter was a really nice, considerate person. He had a few flaws, but don't we all have some? So when I moved in mid-August to Birmingham, where he lived, we officially became a couple. Walter was ready to become a husband, and I was thrilled that with him, I could have what I'd always dreamed of. The two of us being together just made sense to me. We could do life together, hold one another during hard times, knowingly smile at one another during the good, and have babies. I thought I was safe. I would never have to worry about him breaking my heart. So on December 26, in my mama's living room, he asked me to be his wife and I happily said yes. Later that day, I confidently said to Mama, "I told you I was getting married soon!" We both slapped hands and laughed hysterically.

I basically had our wedding planned on the Knot, a wedding website, three months before Walter popped the question. All that was needed to move forward was the proposal. We settled on a morning wedding in August and figured out most of the other details before February.

Other than the thirty percent markup when you mention the word *wedding*, planning wasn't so bad. However, we had some issues on the journey to happily ever after. The biggest one involved issues with his mama and our guest list. Walter hated anything that remotely seemed like a disagreement and tried to get me to come to an understanding with her. From previous experience, I knew it was best for him to handle things with his mama and for me to deal with mine. Premarital counseling confirmed that it was both of our jobs to protect the other when it came to issues with our families. Walter just wanted the two most important women in his world to get along, and neither of us was being easy on him. The tension grew, came to a head, and settled. I was grateful.

Walter and I went through a wave of emotions that summer: I was diagnosed with fibromyalgia, my great-grandmother died, and I had to buy a new car. Together we pushed through and pledged our lives to each other on August 7.

We spent our honeymoon on a cruise to Mexico. The week was blissful as we slept, took a ton of pictures, made beautiful memories, and ate until our bellies hurt. As we exited the ship at the end of our week with sun-kissed skin and linked hands, I hoped we'd remember how much fun we'd had and how much we loved each other in that moment.

Marriage held a lot of adjustments for both of us. We said we wouldn't be that couple arguing over frivolous matters such as whether the ketchup should go in the fridge or the cabinet. We didn't fuss about condiments, but we did quarrel about me not being able to sleep without the fan on and him not being able to sleep without the TV blasting. This resulted in a three-day disagreement, which in turn caused Walter to pull out the air mattress in the living room.

The text messages and emails I was used to getting from him throughout the day dwindled down. When I voiced my concerns to him, he suggested I get a hobby. I took up crocheting but felt disregarded. We were newlyweds, so I thought we should have spent more time nurturing our marriage. I was prideful and micromanaging, and he was passive aggressive. Instead of taking my concerns to God, I tried to fix Walter myself. Didn't I know you can't change a person? But I tried anyway.

CHAPTER ELEVEN

Lately — *Stevie Wonder*

By our first anniversary, we experienced Walter's layoff from his job and fell out of and back in love again. I truly understood that you marry not just a person but that person's entire family. We needed our anniversary trip to Tennessee. During that weekend, we reflected on the previous year, refocused, and connected in a way we hadn't in months. Within weeks, Walter received two offers for a job and we began to pursue becoming homeowners.

In late August, my life got a little more interesting after I accidentally wandered into a leadership meeting for the women's ministry at my new church in Birmingham. It took about three minutes after sitting down to realize I wasn't supposed to be there, but I didn't want to be disruptive so I just stayed in my seat. When the meeting came to a conclusion, I pulled Pastor Enid aside and apologized for crashing. Her next words forever changed my life.

"Oh, I'm so glad you were in here. It was no mistake. You think you're teaching Zumba, but God is getting you ready for women's ministry."

I'd been teaching Zumba at the church since I'd gotten licensed a few months before, and Pastor Enid attended my class regularly. At her words, I laughed and told her she'd missed God on this one. She laughed as well but didn't waiver from her statement. For the next couple of weeks, her words were confirmed by other leaders in my life.

At a church service in early October, I got my first vision ever as Pastor Sean prophesied over different sections of the church. I saw myself on a stage with as many women as I could see from left to right; none of them had on Zumba clothes. Immediately, I bent all the way over and began to hyperventilate. I'd heard about people who experienced God in crazy ways, but never did I think I'd be one of them. I was terrified and couldn't talk about what I'd seen for weeks without crying. There was no way to know this was just the beginning of what God had in store for me.

Several weeks after the vision, I boarded a plane for the first time in ten years with four girlfriends to head to Texas. We were headed there to attend the Woman Thou Art Loosed Conference. It was the most life-changing event I'd ever attended. All the speakers allowed God to use them to light a fire in twenty-five thousand souls. I'd never heard women preach with such power and confidence. I arrived home ready to purse the nudge I was feeling in my heart about women's ministry, but I had no idea how.

Lately —Stevie Wonder

Over the phone, Chrishauna and I discussed what we should do. We both agreed that we should hold a women's meeting, that every woman should bring a dish, and that no subject was untouchable; the gathering was to be a safe space. The goal was to create what I'd longed for but never seen.

Both of our worlds had been rocked by Woman Thou Art Loosed, but we thought it would be a good idea to involve some more experienced women. So Chrishauna contacted her cousin Juanica, and I called Tanya. Both of these women were spiritual mentors. Juanica had been in ministry for years and was an inspiration to me every time I was in her presence. Tanya attended church with me, and I'd been getting close to her over the past year. After getting everyone on board, we set the date for November 18 and I sent out an Evite to all the email addresses I had.

Walter and I were getting settled in the new house we'd just bought, I was embarking on ministry, and something clicked. We were still at this place I couldn't quite figure out, and it disturbed me. Roommates would have been a more accurate description of us than husband and wife. I thought that when all the transition came to an end, things would get better.

To try to bridge the gap, I talked to Walter several times about how I was feeling and took a break from Zumba class for a week. Walter brushed off all conversations as if what I was sensing wasn't a big deal. He also reminded me that he hadn't asked me to take off from Zumba. His nonchalant behavior about our marriage and his erratic attitude mixed with my mouth began to turn our home into a war zone.

Tanya sensed something was bothering me. I told her, "You know how you can drop kids off at the fire station and they don't question or look for the parents? Well, I want to pack up Walter's book bag with both of his laptops, some clean clothes, and a snack and drop him off at the nearest station."

My confession caught her off guard, but she chuckled and advised me to keep pursuing my husband in a godly way. I was doing my best to hold my peace, but I felt as if he were doing the Cha-Cha Slide all over my nerves. I couldn't figure out what was going on with him.

The week of November 14, we had a huge blowout the night before Walter headed to Chicago for training with his job. It was so bad that he slept in the basement. I didn't really sleep that night because of the tears. We barely mumbled a word to one another before I left for work that morning. Walter texted me late that night to let me know he'd arrived in Chicago, but I'd known hours before from Facebook when he'd checked in.

I was at my wits' end, so the next day, I got the phone number of the counselor a coworker suggested for just about everything and set up an appointment that upcoming weekend. After confirming the details, I texted Walter, "We're going to counseling on Sunday at 2:00 p.m. with Dr. Patricia Hamilton." This text started a two-hour conversation about fault and blame. I didn't hear from him again for three days.

Lately —Stevie Wonder

The day of his return flight, I told him I didn't think he needed to be visible while Girl Talk (the get-together Chrishauna and I had planned) was going on at our home that night. Walter gave an excuse about being tired from training and not wanting to be restricted from coming and going in our house.

He'd known for weeks about the women coming that evening. I didn't have the energy to fuss with him, but I asked him not to get a hotel room as he'd threatened. I was beginning to feel drained but pushed my personal issues to the back of my mind as I prepared for what lay ahead later that night.

I was excited all day at work. Women started showing up a little before 7:00 p.m. I couldn't believe the turnout. It looked like Thanksgiving dinner as our group of twenty circled up to bless all the food we'd brought for the occasion.

After we ate, the conversation began. We all tuned in as the more seasoned women answered the questions about life, love, and God. After an hour, one young lady raised her hand to speak. She told us she didn't feel worthy of anything good and contemplated suicide all the time. The atmosphere in the room shifted completely. We all gathered around this woman, spoke life over her, and then went into battle, not with fists or weapons but with prayer.

Her confession was like an avalanche. Women all over the room exposed their wounds, and we covered them with God's word. When the last woman left at 1:30 a.m., I knew that this is what God created me to do. I finally let every word that had been spoken over me regarding ministry settle in my innermost parts and gave God my yes, not with my lips but in my heart.

Walter had sneaked into the basement while the women and I were still upstairs, so I woke him up and we went to bed. The next day, I couldn't stop talking about everything that happened the night before, and he seemed genuinely happy for me. He put our new kitchen table together as we watched college football and I prepared dinner. The next day, we went to church, grabbed a quick bite, and headed to our counseling session.

I knew Walter expected me to talk on and on about all his faults and failures. If I hadn't recognized I had just as many shortcomings within our union, I would have. Instead of mentioning our issues collectively, I told Dr. Hamilton I wanted to figure out why I had certain tendencies. I wanted to understand why I was the way I was. For the majority of the hour, we discussed my relationships with my parents growing up. It was only a short time, yet my outer shell came off and some of the troubles from my childhood were revealed. I cried during our session, on the way home, and in Walter's arms as we lay down for a nap. Before we'd left our appointment, Dr. Hamilton had advised him not to try to fix my tears but just be there for me, and he was.

I woke up from my nap about four hours later and could hear Walter moving around in our basement. Rested, I got up and decided to find a new Zumba routine on YouTube to learn for class the next day. I started searching

Lately —Stevie Wonder

for where I'd put my laptop but decided to use Walter's iPad instead because the internet worked faster on it. After I found the iPad, I settled back on the bed and opened the browser.

I paused. Walter hadn't called me once while he was in in Chicago, so I had no idea what he'd done there. I opened up his Gmail account, looking for nothing in particular, and was about to close it as the title of an email caught my eye: "Horny in a hotel."

Wow. So maybe this will explain what's been going on with my husband for the last few months. I took a deep breath and allowed my finger to click on the email, but I wasn't prepared for what I read.

Date: 2011-11-17 Time: 1:33 a.m.

Sexy blk male from Alabama. Horny in the hotel. I'm a top, looking for a sexy TS or TG to pound. 5-11, 230, muscular

CHAPTER TWELVE

Gravity —*John Mayer*

I squinted as I read the email several times, but it didn't change the words on the screen. Walter had placed an ad on Craigslist early Tuesday morning, and the responses he'd received were being sent to his email account.

TS or TG. Wait! My heart plunged to the pit of my stomach, and my mouth dropped in disbelief. *This can't be right!* I'd taken a sexual inequality class in college, so I knew what the abbreviations stood for. *Transsexual or transgender? "I'm a top"? The man I married is gay?*

I closed my eyes and collected myself before I began forwarding the ad and all the responses to several of my email addresses. As I read the responses, I saw the conversations between him and the men who'd taken interest in his post, but nowhere did I see he'd actually met up with anyone. That didn't mean he hadn't met a random guy on the streets and had sex with him.

After I finished, I calmly got off the bed and walked down to our basement, where Walter was playing on his Xbox. How I remained calm was nothing but Jesus. I strategically sat down on the couch across from where he was seated and asked him what he did while he was in Chicago. I wanted to see every breath and eye flutter as he was confronted with the truth. Walter began describing the food he'd eaten and the people he'd met in training and even explained some of the things he'd learned.

"Why didn't you call me while you were there?"

"We weren't getting along, Torrie, and I didn't want to argue with you."

"Oh, okay." Pause. "I saw the ad you put on Craigslist."

I'd never seen a man so scared and calm at the same time. Several moments went by before he asked, "What ad?"

"I'll go get your iPad," I responded. "Stay right here."

I walked up to our room, grabbed his iPad, and headed back to the basement. Before I could get all the way off the bottom step, he snatched the iPad out of my hands.

My mind was finally catching up with what I'd just discovered. "Not again, God! Why *this*?" I screamed.

I turned and walked back up the stairs with Walter close on my heels. As I walked down the hallway to get my suitcase, I began to cry and have a conversation with myself as he talked to my back. I kept repeating, "Oh, my God!" Then I said, "Torrie, this is not your fault."

"Do you feel better that it's not your fault?"

That was it. I turned around and began swinging at Walter's head with everything I had. "You could have killed

Gravity —John Mayer

us! You like men and you let us buy this house!" I got angrier with every passing second. I swung harder. Walter covered his head to protect himself.

After I ran out of breath, I went into the closet in our second bedroom and dragged my suitcase into our bedroom. Unconsciously, I began opening drawers and throwing clothes into the suitcase. I had no idea where I was going, but I had to get out of there. I was a furious ball of emotion, and one of us might not live to see daylight. It was more than likely going to be Walter.

Fifteen months. That's how far I was into my marriage with Cedric when I caught him with his girlfriend. And it was fifteen months into my marriage with Walter when I found the emails.

As horrible as this was, everything made sense. My normally calm, kind, stable-minded husband had become erratic and irritable. He'd put an ad on a public forum soliciting sex from a man dressed like a woman. God knew how long he'd been doing similar things. My mind flipped back to the job he'd had at the beginning of our relationship—the job that had made him travel once a month out of state.

Females I could handle. Life had taught me that things wouldn't always be easy and even your most treasured loved ones will hurt you unintentionally at some point. But this . . . how was I going to begin to navigate through this? My life as I'd known it would never be the same.

After spending the night at a friend's house, I stepped back into our house the next morning. It felt nothing like a home, much less my home. I called into work and scheduled an emergency appointment with my gynecologist. Then I called Juanica and Tanya to tell them what was going on. All I could tell Tanya over the phone was that the situation was bad and that she had to come over.

As I recounted the memories of the night before, she pulled me into her arms. It took everything in me not to stop breathing altogether.

"We will get through this, Torrie. I promise. And I will support you, no matter what you decide."

I hadn't thought far enough ahead to consider having a choice. I was too consumed with the pain, but I definitely had a million things to think about.

I gathered myself together by six to make it out to my church to teach Zumba. I really tried to give my students a great class, but I knew I'd failed as my student and fellow church member Elainia stood in front of me, asking what was wrong. I pulled her into a side room before my mind caught up with my words and I admitted to her that I'd had to go get tested earlier for what my husband may or may not have exposed me to.

Before I knew it, Elainia wrapped her arms around me and prayed one of the most heartfelt prayers I'd ever heard. I'd never experienced someone hugging me and taking grief off of me, but that's what happened. Elainia didn't let my pain be solely mine as she cried with me and promised to hold my hand though this process.

Over the next three days, I experienced so many different emotions. Walter had taken up residence in the basement, so we barely saw one another, but we did talk through text messages. He claimed he'd never slept with a man and wasn't interested in them, but he did admit he had been masturbating and been addicted to pornography for years. He alleged that the turbulent atmosphere at home sent him to Craigslist late that night to post the ad and claimed he'd picked up the lingo for his own post by looking at others on the website. I threatened to expose his secret to his family, friends, and social media. I made up names to call him after I got tired of typing the same insults.

After I ranted to Walter, God said to me, clear as day, "He's my child too, so you can't talk to him like that." There were very few times I could remember God speaking to me clearly, so I stopped the name-calling and came apart silently.

Due to our dilemma, we didn't spend Thanksgiving with either of our families. I wasn't sure I could put up a façade that everything was okay, so we spent Thanksgiving alone together in our picture-perfect house that had crumbled on the inside.

Do you know what it feels like to experience the highest high and the lowest low at the same time?

While I was praying about what to call the gathering of women we were going to have at my house, God confirmed the name Beloved. I prayed for a couple of weeks about different names, but peace settled in my spirit about Beloved. It means "prized, cherished, adored, precious, and treasured."[1] I wanted every woman who walked through my door to understand that God felt that way about her no matter what she'd been through. I declared my living room a safe space and between the women giving the word for that night, open discussion, and prayer, something phenomenal was happening: they were becoming empowered and being freed from the junk in their lives.

It had never been a desire of mine to become a speaker, but that's what I was doing monthly. I doubted myself and my knowledge of the Word and wondered if I was hearing God correctly, but He affirmed me every step of the way. I had no ministerial training, yet I was being used as a messenger. Was I perfect? Absolutely not, but I couldn't recall anything that matched the fulfilment I experienced afterward.

On the other hand, I had moments when I felt nothing at all and moments when I felt as if I were being suffocated. Walter and I had a weekly appointment with Dr. Hamilton as we tried to make sense of our lives after the big discovery. For a while, I didn't feel anything. This nothingness concerned me, so I mentioned it to Dr. Hamilton in one of our sessions. She explained how the stages of grief were relevant to what I experienced and that I was probably in denial.

The uncertainty of my marriage knocked me to my knees and caused me to seek God as never before. My struggle was the logic that gay men don't marry women; they pursue relationships with men. And since I was never able to confirm that Walter had been with a man, I didn't know what to think.

We'd made a covenant to one another. We'd bought a house together. I wanted to believe that no man would do this to a woman, but I couldn't help but think in the back of my mind that Walter had attempted to fix his desire for men by marrying me.

Because I was trying to be a reformed hothead, I allowed God direct me on when to speak and when to remain silent. We had three bedrooms upstairs in our house, and I decided one of them would be my designated quiet time area. My girlfriend Ashley Talley told me about an acronym she'd learned in ministry school, H.A.L.T. It stands for *hurting*, *angry*, *lonely*, and *tired*. I thought the meaning was genius, so that's what I called my prayer room. My H.A.L.T. room was a refuge for me, not just with this mess with Walter but for every aspect of my life. I was moving beyond spiritual calisthenics and crossing over to deep understanding and true relationship.

As my denial began to fade, all I felt was immense sadness. The fact that my husband wanted something I could not physically give him slammed into me. Dr. Hamilton was trying her best to help us unravel the pieces of our lives, but it was hard. Some days, I left her office feeling we had a chance; other days, I felt it was only a matter of time before all that was underneath erupted.

During one of sessions, Walter admitted he felt God had been trying to get his attention about masturbating. Walter said that every time he'd done it, something bad would happen. He mentioned being in a car wreck the previous summer, getting laid off, and having huge fights with me after he'd gratified himself.

"I would decide if we could afford an argument or something going wrong as to whether I would masturbate or not."

"Did you masturbate while we were trying to get the house?"

"No."

"So you knew God was trying to get you to stop, and instead you played Russian Roulette with our marriage?"

I packed a suitcase when I got home but sank down onto the floor before I zipped it up. Where would I go? I felt trapped. I wasn't ready to admit to my friends and family what was really going on.

Walter became irritated when I cried, and I got angry that he had the nerve to feel anything besides regret for the tears he'd caused. "I'm trying, Torrie," he said over and over. It didn't feel that way. And my strength regarding the matter was nearly depleted, so I stopped questioning him.

Our focus shifted from us to our loved ones when, between our families, we experienced three deaths within two months. One of Walter's teenage cousins died. I'd never seen him so vulnerable. He was overcome with grief, but I could barely stand allowing him to hug me. I couldn't let him in. I spent countless nights on the floor in H.A.L.T. because I knew neither the endless apologies, the good behavior, nor any of Walter's polished words could heal me.

In my weakness, I got undone only in front of God. I would stay on the floor until it didn't hurt anymore, until my body shook and all the tears I owned became one with the carpet. The beautiful exchange, as I called it, became

Gravity —John Mayer

my ritual. I exchanged my questioning, pain, and doubt for God's assurance, love and peace.

Then my great-aunt Diane died. Her death brought about a shift in my family. In addition to that, my sister Jessica and one of Diane's sons were at each other's throats due to a verbal fight a week before Diane died. Discord spread throughout our relatives.

All of it came to a head after the funeral at the repass. It was bad enough the family was divided, but now that division was being played out in front of our entire hometown. Blows were almost thrown and curse words hung deeply in the air. Diane wasn't even covered in the ground before our family was torn apart completely.

The war didn't stop there. It continued for weeks on social media and in public places. After an incident with one of Diane's sons and Jessica, I was on the phone telling my mama that she needed to stop her part of the foolishness on social media. To defend her actions, Mama blurted out my cousin's choice words to my sister: "That's why my stepdaddy ****** your sister!"

If I told you it didn't feel as if the world had stopped spinning, I'd be lying. Everything turned white, and I stopped dead in my tracks. "Wait, he said that?" I asked Mama. She replied yes. That was only the first time it was said in public. It was what they said in order to rip the scab off a deep, scandalous wound.

I had nothing to do with the disagreement and remained neutral. My concern was what was right. When it came down to it, everyone was hurting and broken.

Instead of reaching for one another for comfort, we commenced a battle no one actually won. All parties, both perpetrators and innocent bystanders, were injured.

As bitterness tried to take root, I gave it to God and began to travel back in time twenty years to address some of the circumstances surrounding the molestation. I wanted answers from Mama and needed healing from God. Yes, the words that fell from my cousin's lips were careless, but they ended up thrusting me into healing and forgiveness.

Mama and I sat down, and she explained the memory I had of the cuts on her hands that had appeared days after my abuse was revealed. She'd attacked Diane because Diane had waited several days to tell Mama about what she'd walked in on Trey doing to me. Also Diane had thought sending Trey back to his hometown would be enough to keep Mama from calling the police. Mama explained how she'd stopped LPN school because she was afraid of Jessica and me being out of her sight and how another aunt convinced her to finish the program.

She explained how the words she'd spoke over me two decades earlier haunted her and that she could never forget what she'd said. In that moment, I began to truly realize that your parents can only give you what they have, nothing more. Mama had been just as wounded by the selfish acts of the pedophile who took my innocence in the back room of a house as I was. I didn't want to allow pieces of me to die just because the crash course in life called pain happened. I wanted to stretch myself to move beyond it and trust in the resurrection power of Jesus' blood.

Gravity — John Mayer

Just as I was scraping the surface of my past, Walter's behavior got strange again. No, he hadn't disappeared for hours or made questionable phone calls, but his entire demeanor changed. He was acting exactly how he'd acted before the infidelity came out. Everything in me wanted to brush my feelings off, but my intuition kicked in. I petitioned God and sought advice from the circle of women I allowed into this area of our lives.

On the way to work soon after, I called Walter and asked him if he was cheating on me, watching pornography, or masturbating. He answered no to all three questions. I then asked him to get tested for HIV. Walter didn't outright refuse to get tested, but he did want to know what it would prove if he did. Dr. Hamilton had stated that his getting tested would give us the possibility of a new start. Every time I asked Walter if he'd gotten tested, he responded no.

I started having anxiety attacks from the stress of everything. When I discussed the attacks with Walter, he pointed the finger at everyone else but himself: "Your ex-husband and old relationships are to blame. None of this has to do with me. Your mom and family issues are the problem."

My hair thinned and began to fall out. I had headaches for days and found out my blood pressure was dangerously high. Here I was trying to press our way through the mess and be a decent wife, and all I was getting was pushback from Walter.

Tanya held me accountable in the hope that even infidelity would work out for our good. Walter didn't have anyone in his life making sure he was staying on the right path. Walter was too ashamed of what he'd done to confide in anyone. He did talk to Tanya's husband a couple of times but didn't stay in touch with him. Walter felt as if he had nothing to prove to me, and I believe he came to the conclusion that I wasn't going to leave him. But I was devastated and on my way to becoming bald.

In early July, I pulled my pastor aside one Sunday after service and told him about my marriage. At that point, Pastor Sean had been our shepherd for two years. He'd married us and believed in all God had for us. When I finished telling him what happened, Pastor Sean looked at me, not with pity but with endearment and concern, and said, "I'm so sorry, daughter."

I absolutely lost it and let everything going on in my head and heart roll down my face. Pastor Sean promised to schedule lunch with Walter that week and do what he could to help us through this. I didn't mention the conversation I'd had with our pastor to Walter. He would find out soon enough.

The next night, I had another anxiety attack. I lay in bed sweating, out of breath, and consumed with fear, but eventually I drifted off to sleep. Walter came up from the basement later and, seeing the perspiration on my face, asked if I was okay. I explained what had happened, and he placed his hands on my back and prayed. After I was done getting ready for work the next morning, I asked him if he still thought the anxiety had nothing to do with him.

Gravity — John Mayer

As he fumbled to deflect his role in the situation, I allowed eight months of frustration to break loose for ten minutes straight. I called him a failure, threw every possible insult concerning homosexuality at him, and told him the only he did right was screw up our marriage.

Once I was finished empting out every crevice of pain onto him, I went to work. After getting settled and working up the nerve, I sent my friend Erica a message and asked if I could come stay at her house for a while. We'd met at UA and become friends and later pledged Delta together. She said yes, and I was grateful. I didn't have any family in town, not that I would have considered staying with them. I just needed to get away while I made a decision to stick this marriage out or walk away.

As I packed up my car later that night, I confessed to Pastor Enid that I felt as if God had truly forsaken me. God had shown me my purpose through Beloved, but I felt I'd lost my husband despite all my efforts. I didn't walk away when many would have, and I didn't blast him on social media. Prayer had become my anchor, and I'd become submissive to more seasoned woman, not just for ministry but with my personal life as well so I could be the best version of Torrie I was able to be. I'd fasted to rid myself of selfishness with the expectation of hearing God on a new level. But Walter had done nothing except try to act as if he didn't have a problem. All I felt was despair, and I felt as if God had dropped me and left me to make the best out of my life given the circumstances.

Pastor Enid prayed, cried with me, and agreed that my decision to move out for a while was probably best for Walter and me. I figured I would explain to Walter that we needed space for the time being, but he never came home that night. He didn't call me and I didn't call him either. I had no idea it was my last night under our roof.

CHAPTER THIRTEEN

Gone Already — Faith Evans

It was amazing to me that in just a few months, I didn't recognize any aspect of my life. My heart grew cold. Anger and bitterness colored my words and actions. At first, I sought relief in God, but when things got worse, I shifted blame from Walter to Him. None of this had been included in the vision I'd gotten last October. I'd started Beloved and prayerfully begun ministry school earlier that summer, but now the very thought of continuing anything in God's name made me furious.

I looked for peace in the bottom of wine bottles and the sleep that was never restful, no matter how much of it I had. Nothing was working. Holding it together truly became a show; I had to prep myself to do anything involving people.

Walter and I met with our pastors again, and I'm sure it was only respect for them that kept us from screaming at each other in their presence. At the end of our session, we were given the assignment to contact one another and talk. Walter didn't even try to hold up his end of the agreement. Two weeks after I'd moved out, I told him I didn't want to be married anymore. Then Walter finally got tested and left the HIV-negative test results in my car while I was at work.

With my attitude and incomplete plans for Walter's upcoming birthday, it didn't take long for Mama to figure out something was wrong. I'd been dodging her for days, so when she called early one morning while I was on my way to work, I admitted to her that I'd moved out. I told her about Walter's possible infidelity in Chicago, masturbation, and pornography, but I didn't mention the men.

Mama was crushed by the revelation. Since she knew, I figured it would be best to tell Daddy and his second wife, Jennifer, whom he'd married two years earlier. My parents cried with me and offered every way they could to make the situation a bit easier for me. I've never been so relieved I didn't have to act as if everything was fine in my world, but I didn't want any of them to worry about me.

Jennifer and Daddy's concern went to another level while she and I were on the phone the next day. Jennifer wanted to know why I'd pushed so hard for Walter to get tested. "It's not like he's cheated on you with men," she said. I remained silent as she made the same statement again. The saying "Silence speaks louder than words" was only true for the few seconds it took the stillness on my end to register with Jennifer's brain. Then she screamed so loud that the hairs on my arms stood up.

Erica, the friend I was staying with, had guessed it a few weeks before. I'd mentioned the Craigslist ad to her, but not its contents. Two nights later, when we went to dinner, she told me not to lie to her and asked if Walter had been looking for sex from men on the Internet. When I asked her how she knew, she stated it was too easy for men to cheat. Posting an ad on the World Wide Web seemed to be a lot of effort for a man in a city for only a few days.

Everyone who knew the whole truth was advised not to even hint about the revelation in front of Mama. Like most mothers, she was beyond protective of her children. There wasn't anything she wouldn't do to those who intentionally harmed Jessica and me. I preferred for her to stay out of jail, so every time I told someone about Walter's possible relationships with men, I made sure that person knew that what really went down didn't need to be mentioned to her.

Several days later, in an attempt to talk like adults, Walter and I met at a local park. He complained that he felt as if I'd given up on us when I decided to move out of our home. I let him know that just because he'd remained a resident of our house didn't mean his heart was there. To me, he'd mentally checked out of our house before we'd ever moved in. I told him I felt as if he'd had an interest in men before he and I ever met and that he'd tried to fix himself by marrying me. After telling me yet again he didn't like men and never had, Walter got up from the bench and walked away. I wasn't convinced, and for a good reason.

Everything came to a head on our second anniversary, a couple of days later. Walter called before I woke up and left a voicemail expressing his love for me and wishing me a happy anniversary. We'd planned to go to dinner that night, and my goal was simply getting through it without insulting him. In an attempt to have a decent tone, I didn't return his call until 10:00 a.m. He was unaware I was off work and had sent a dozen roses to my job. I told him I'd stop by to get them after running some errands.

Holly, my friend from college, called to check on me midway through the day. She didn't hesitate to let me know I sounded worse each time she talked to me. I admitted I was allowing myself to be in my feelings because I felt Walter had duped me into marrying him while secretly indulging in an alternate lifestyle.

While we were talking, I decided to go to the house, check the mail, and grab a few things. The first thing I saw when I walked into the basement was a box for a prepaid phone on the couch. I thought to myself that that was odd, but I trekked up the stairs while Holly tried to convince me Walter wasn't gay. She always tried to see the good in people, and for my sake, she didn't want it to be true. I made my way to our bedroom and found a phone plugged into the wall. It wasn't the phone I knew Walter to have, so I figured it was the phone from the box I'd seen downstairs.

My conversation with Holly continued as I placed her on speaker, but my attention shifted to trying to get into the mystery phone. After fumbling with it a bit before getting in, I scrolled first through the call log, which was empty, and then through the text messages. I was about to dismiss the messages in the phone as spam until I read what one of them said.

"You've subscribed to InterActive Male-Msg Alerts . . . "
Date: 08/03/2012

Unaware of what InterActive Male was, I pulled up Google on my phone and typed the name in the search bar. It was a gay male chat site. What I'd felt all along was true. The Craigslist ad in Chicago wasn't an isolated incident. Walter had sworn he was making an effort to save our marriage, but here he was seeking men out on the Internet.

All of the air in my lungs exited my body as I described to Holly what I'd just found. "Do you still think he's not gay?" I asked her as I took pictures of my new findings. After gathering evidence of the texts, I sent the photos to all my email accounts and gave Holly my passwords and usernames in case something happened when I confronted Walter. I wanted to be cautious; I knew scared people hurt people. I had no idea how Walter would act once the truth was staring him in the face.

"You need to come home," I told Walter after I'd hung up with Holly. He said he was on his way. I slipped his phone into my pocket and repositioned a chair in the living room to allow me to see our bedroom door down the hall, as well as the basement stairs. Fifteen minutes later, he walked in and said happy anniversary.

"Have you seen any bugs? I set off a b—" He took off down the hall toward our bedroom. When he came back a few seconds later, he asked, "Where's my phone?"

I handed it to him, sucked in all the air my lungs could hold, and said sincerely, "Let's forget I'm your wife, and you tell me honestly how long you've been interested in men."

"I don't know what you're talking about," he said as he pushed buttons on his phone.

"Walter! I saw the messages in the phone!"

"What messages?"

"The ones you probably just erased. Let me see it."

Walter handed me the phone. I looked, and of course he'd erased every text. I pushed the phone back into his hands. "As long as you keep denying that you have a problem, you are never going to get the healing that you need."

We continued to talk. For a few seconds, I saw remorse, sorrow, and shame in his eyes. It was the most transparent he'd been in the last nine months.

"Torrie, I need your help."

Maybe if he'd said this sooner, we wouldn't have been there experiencing such a raw moment. It was too late to save anything. I replied, "You need a cover up, and I'm not gonna be that for you anymore."

The conversation went from decent to worse: when he asked if we were still going to dinner, I laughed as hard I could in his face. It was at this moment I realized he really thought I wanted a husband so much that I would ignore this situation. Had I fueled his thoughts while we were dating to the point where he thought I wouldn't exit a toxic marriage? Maybe I had. Happily ever after had consumed my thoughts, and when he came along, I willingly got onto this rollercoaster ride.

"It's over, Walter." Then I threatened to stop by his mom's house and tell her the truth about him.

He responded, "If you mess up my social life, I'm gonna show you something!"

Needless to say, we didn't share dinner or exchange gifts, and neither of us mentioned our big day in a positive way to anyone. Even with what I'd known before August 7, I'd still expected God to intervene and make everything right for us. I'd woken up that day as a woman who had a small glimmer of hope that just maybe her marriage would be restored. I would lie down that night knowing I was ending another lifelong relationship.

Pride wouldn't allow me to wallow in regret, pain, or uncertainty. That night I put on a dress, curled my hair, put on makeup, and took my old roommate Jenn out to eat sushi. What had been had ended, and what would be would soon present itself. As my eyes closed that night, I was glad I finally knew: Our test wouldn't turn into our testimony.

After I returned from a Zumba convention a week later, my mind went into an autopilot mode named "Get out of the marriage." Within two weeks, I paid a divorce lawyer in full and put our house on the market.

To say that Walter was being difficult would be an understatement. He'd promised the week before to be cooperative, but when he realized I really was moving forward with the divorce, he became problematic. He sent me articles about the long-term effects of divorce, but I still proceeded to move forward. He broke down and told me he couldn't afford the mortgage and his health insurance, which covered prescriptions he needed, if we divorced at that time.

I responded, "Well, you are going to die, then! If you think I'm going to stay in this to convenience you, you have me messed up! You should have thought about that before you decided to whore around!"

The following week, he began to make excuses about not having time to meet with a notary to sign the paperwork. After logging off of my phone at work and scooting into a corner in my cubicle, I called and reminded him that I didn't need his signature to get a divorce, but if I had to pay more money to get out, the reason for ending our union on the paperwork was going to change from "irreconcilable differences" to "unusual sexual behavior." I reminded him that divorce decrees were public records and that his parents, family, friends, and coworkers could Google it to see why I'd left him. He agreed to meet with me that upcoming Sunday.

After the paperwork was signed, I began to focus on getting settled by looking for an apartment. Normalcy was something I craved, but all the stress was taking a toll on my body. My weight dropped drastically, and breaking out in hives every other week became routine. A trip to my family doctor helped get me back on track. After I'd explained my life for the last ten months, Dr. Ricketts suggested I take anxiety medicine to take the edge off of my nerves. I voiced my concern about the horror stories I'd heard about addiction to those types of prescriptions. He explained that my current health issues would more than likely disappear once I began the regimen he'd suggested. When I continued to complain, he said in a raised tone, "Take the medicine, daughter!" We had that type of relationship with one another.

Within days, I felt better, my mood stabilized, and the hives went away for good. For the next couple of months until I stopped taking the medicine, I had a standing appointment every two weeks with Dr. Ricketts.

I was sitting in my room at Erica's rolling my hair when she knocked on the door. In a serious tone she said, "I have something to tell you." Erica admitted that several weeks ago, she'd told Lauren, one of our sorority sisters, why I'd left Walter. She then went on to explain that Lauren had a friend who went on a date with him. After finding out who he was, Lauren supposedly told only her friend, "Don't date him. I heard he was gay." As Erica concluded the story, she shrugged and said, "Well, I just had to tell somebody."

I didn't know what stung worse: her betrayal or her excuse for telling my business. I considered Erica one of my best friends, and she was telling the secret I hadn't wanted to admit to her in the first place. When I'd told her, she'd been very opinionated about how she thought I should handle the situation with Walter. She'd even confessed that she questioned our friendship because she hadn't been made aware of my marriage issues sooner. My own mother didn't know the full truth, yet my friend felt jaded that she didn't know what was going on in my marriage. The conversation lasted almost two hours, and I made sure I told Erica that I didn't owe anyone an explanation about my life.

After another discussion two days later, I moved out. I was at a crossroads. I could indulge in the sadness or press forward. The latter won. My heart had begun to soften toward God, and I'd started attending church again a few weeks earlier. I knew this issue with Erica was an attack from the enemy to take me over the edge. I stayed with Chrishauna until I could move into my place at the end of the month.

Over the next several weeks, I saw my brother get married, settled into my new apartment, and attended Woman Thou Art Loosed in Atlanta with Jessica and Mama. The trip to the conference was right on time as I worshiped and cried my heart out in what seemed like a sea of women. So much had happened in the last few months; I needed a radical encounter with God, and that's exactly what I got.

It was also great to experience it with my two sidekicks. While we were waiting at a restaurant for our food after leaving a session, Mama told me, "I don't know what all Walter put you through, but on the other side, you are gonna be unstoppable!" She went on to describe what she believed my life would look like in ten years. As I wiped the tears out of my eyes, I only nodded, yet my mind said what my lips didn't: I was going to make it.

As I began to heal and press into the Savior's presence, I started to hear the Holy Spirit whisper, "Beloved." It had been six months since the last Beloved, and if I was honest, I missed it dearly. On the first Friday in November, around ten women and I gathered in my living room to start the ministry back up again. It felt truly amazing to be operating in purpose again. Toni, one of my sorors, came for the first time. We started a beautiful friendship before she moved to South Carolina.

Everything was moving along fine until I noticed some pain on my right side. I went to one doctor, who misdiagnosed me. Another trip to a doctor revealed I had a kidney stone. I hate the saying "If it ain't one thing, it's another!" but this was ringing true around every corner I turned. Here I was feeding my faith, which in return starved my fears, so Satan had to go attack my body. After a couple of failed attempts to get the stone to pass on its own, my surgery to remove it was scheduled for December 3. I can't even say I was sad about that. I felt as if this was just another lesson I was learning: to praise God even in bad times.

Meanwhile, I was gearing up to celebrate my birthday. On December 1, I was able to sit at a table surrounded by friends and family. My life had completely transformed through the last year, and I was grateful to be thriving through it all.

The next day, Jessica and I went to Sunday morning service at the Summit Church at Birmingham to support the church's founder, Pastor Pat, as he released a new book. At the end of a life-changing message, he told us, "Close your eyes and imagine the worst moment of your life. Then imagine Jesus coming out of the wall and saying, 'I was there with you all along.'" I remembered sitting on my bed opening the email that changed everything I knew to be true about my life as a wife. Jesus was there with me. His heart was just as torn up as mine. That message has resonated with me until this day.

I finished the year as strong as I could. My relationship with God was restored, and I was falling more in love with Him by the moment. I'd survived my hell and was ready for all 2013 had in store. When the divorce was finalized in mid-December, I felt as if a boulder had been lifted from my shoulders. I could finally move forward.

CHAPTER FOURTEEN

Man in the Mirror — *Michael Jackson*

On the first day of 2013, I sat on my couch, reminiscing about my life. I was tired of repeating the same cycles and truly wanted to break from all hindrances from my life. As I mentally combed through the years, my memory settled on twenty years before, when I was molested. It was when I remembered everything changing in my world. I decided it was no longer going to be an option to navigate the journey to healing alone.

The next business day, I called Dr. Hamilton and set up an appointment. When I saw her a few days later, I told her we were going to be best friends because I was going to be in her office once a week for the next couple of months. She let me know that digging up and exploring old wounds would be uncomfortable and painful yet worth it. I was committed to becoming who I knew I could be: Whole. Free. Confident. Me.

About three weeks in, Dr. Hamilton told me I had to write my mother a letter, telling her how nine-year- old Torrie felt about what she'd said all those years ago. I told her there was no way I was going to do that and objected for a while. Through our sessions, I'd realized I blamed myself for being molested because of what Mama had said to me. Internally, I was fighting the battle of blame and insecurity and trying to prove I was worthy of love. The words never escaped my lips, but the patterns that came so easily made a different confession. Mama was tough, and I knew that no matter how gently I explained everything, the backlash from her would cause an issue.

My flesh put up a good fight, but eventually my spirit won. It took me a week to pen the letter and send it to her. It's amazing how we swear that we want change but refuse to do the work to achieve the best results in our lives. Our bodies go through withdrawals when we eliminate caffeine and sugar from our diets. We get headaches and our attitudes are less than stellar. But after a while, we have more energy and begin to lose weight. When we stay focused on the goal, we see positive results. It usually gets worse before it gets better.

This definitely rang true with Mama and me. She was never shy about voicing her opinion, and she'd raised Jessica and me to hold our own. When I gave her the letter, Mama snapped, just as I'd predicted, and didn't talk to me for a month. But when she calmed down, she found a counselor for herself. Finally, we were making progress. I was so proud of her.

Beloved was back in full swing and consistently growing. In February, we moved from my place to my friend Jenn's house. I was amazed at how God was expanding the ministry.

Toward the end of February, I called the company that had given Walter and me the loan for the house to get a copy of the taxes paid on it the previous year. After getting the representative to agree to send the statement to my new address, she asked if I wanted to pay the mortgage. It was a couple of days before March and Walter hadn't paid the mortgage? I asked her to double check it. It definitely hadn't been paid. I texted Walter and asked him if he'd made arrangements to pay. He claimed the payment had been taken care of already. Sure enough, when I called the loan company the next morning, a payment had been made after I'd talked to him.

After several texts to Walter, I prayed and asked God to sever this last tie I had to him. The next day, I was convinced God had heard my cry: I received an email that someone wanted to look at the house that Sunday. To ensure the house was in order, I made plans to go over sometime that week to clean.

On Friday, I stopped by my place before heading to the house. I called Kristen and told her my "exciting" plans for the evening, and she asked, "Did you tell him you were stopping by?"

"Do you call your car before you get in it?"

She advised that I let him know I would be stopping by as a courtesy. I disagreed with her but did it anyway. I texted him, "I'll be at the house tonight."

He replied, "Why?"

I didn't feel I needed to explain because I was still a joint owner of the house. After a quick trip to Walmart for cleaning supplies, I made my way to Trussville. I had no idea how crazy my night was about to get.

As soon as I stepped into the basement, a fresh scent hit my nose. When I turned on the lights, I could tell the carpet had been cleaned and vacuumed. Next I glanced around and noticed some suitcases; Walter had been up north for a couple of days. As I made my way upstairs, I saw the floors had been shined. *Hmm. It's not like him to keep the house this clean*, I thought.

In the living room on the fireplace was a balloon arrangement that said "Congratulations" and included a card from a female with sentimental jargon. That didn't bother me. My next discovery did.

In the kitchen on the refrigerator was a love letter to him from someone named Kelly. He'd written her one as well. From the contents of the letter, I could tell she'd been in the house. I paused for a moment because all I saw was red.

My phone was in my hand before I knew it. I left an earful on Walter's voicemail before calling my girlfriend Misha. When she answered, I screamed, "You better talk me down!" After I'd explained my findings, Misha told me to leave. I hung up in her face because she wasn't saying what I wanted to hear.

I began to look around the rest of the house. In the bedroom, I found cards Kelly had given Walter. Trying to find a lighter, I searched between the couches downstairs and in every drawer and crevice I could think of. I was about to give up, thinking I would have to go to the store to buy one, but then I found one. I snatched the letters off the fridge and placed them on the counter before setting them on fire. The flames were a tiny but direct reflection of what was going on inside me. My face was red from screaming into my phone and spilling the details of what I'd discovered.

When Holly called, I made my way to the garage, sat in my car, and cried until I started sweating. I felt so stupid. It seemed nothing in his life had changed while mine had been flipped upside down. Walter was still living in the house we'd purchased together, and to top it all off, he'd brought a female into the house after I'd told him not to. All at once, the emotions I'd removed myself from for months flooded me.

Misha had called several times after I'd hung up on her and decided to come by and check on me when I didn't answer. She talked to me until I agreed to leave. I drove to Jenn's house and waited until I thought Walter would go home. When I stopped by again an hour later, he still wasn't there. I'd just decided to head home when I saw his car pulling into the neighborhood. I turned around and went back to the house. I met him in the driveway and asked him if he'd received the email about someone wanting to look at the house Sunday. He said he had.

"Walter, all I asked was that you didn't bring anyone to the house."

"I didn't agree to that."

"You couldn't even live here without my social security number being on this house. If I want to, I can move back in here today and nobody could stop me!"

"Yeah, move back in and help me pay the mortgage."

"You're *not* paying the mortgage! If I move back in here, I'm not giving you a dime! Don't let me catch your girlfriend in my house! I'm gonna tell her who you really are! Think I'm playing with you?"

By this time, it was after eleven and I was standing in the driveway saying anything and everything that came to my mind. I followed Walter into the garage, where we continued our debate. After asking me what kind of Christian I was, he asked, "How's Beloved?"

Those were the ultimate fighting words. Everything in me wanted to smash my fist against his face, but I settled for almost putting my finger up his nose. "You don't get to ask me about Beloved!" I screamed. "Because of you, there almost was no Beloved!"

Beloved was the closest thing to a baby I had, and I was fiercely protective of it. As Walter walked over to the switch to let the garage door down, I could hear my voice vibrating off the house next door. I'm sure I looked and sounded like a mad woman with sweat rolling down my face. As the moments passed, I became more enraged and began chest bumping him.

I didn't know if Walter figured he'd taken it too far or if he was just over having the conversation with me, but he made his way over to his car, began taking bags out of the trunk, and then walked into the house. After he'd disappeared, I grabbed pictures, golf clubs, and anything else I could get my hands on to throw. I headed to the driveway and saw several garbage bags neatly placed inside and next to the trash cans. I picked the cans up, emptied them on the ground, and began kicking the bags throughout the yard.

Honestly, I thought I'd forgiven Walter. Several months earlier, I'd gotten on my knees before taking communion and wholeheartedly professed forgiveness over our situation. Hating him took too much energy. How could I allow him to dominate my emotions like that? Walter didn't keep our vows, so why did I expect him not to invite anyone into the house where I no longer lived?

I left but came back an hour later to show him I could come and go as I pleased because I was still a joint owner of the house. Before I left for the final time that night, I told him I'd be back the next day to regulate.

CHAPTER FIFTEEN

Strength, Courage, and Wisdom —India Arie

"Where do you want to go, Torrie?"

This was the second time Holly asked me. I wanted to get away. I needed to get away. But I didn't have the money to really go anywhere.

I paused. "Texas."

It was 2:00 a.m. By 10:00 a.m., I was getting off a plane in Dallas.

Holly knew me too well and knew I was going to end up back at that house, act like a fool, and probably end up in jail for real. She bought my plane ticket and got me a rental car and a hotel room for a couple of days. Everybody needs a Holly in their lives!

After getting the arrangements together for my stay in Dallas, I took a deep breath and heard the Holy Spirit say, "Apologize." I texted Walter, "I was totally out of line tonight. I apologize from the bottom of my heart."

When I turned my phone on after I'd landed, I had a message from Walter asking how I thought the night before had gone. Again I admitted I was wrong, but I told him I meant what I'd said about his actions being disrespectful. He told me Kelly was just a friend and he'd grieved our marriage. I explained I couldn't care less about him moving on; I just didn't want his love interest in the house with both our names on it.

For the next three days, I cried, slept, and talked to God. I was open and raw as I wrote in my journal about how humiliated I felt. On Sunday morning, I went to a service at the Potter's House. I could have sworn Bishop Jakes knew everything I'd been going through. He talked about the importance of building on a solid foundation, as Matthew 7 refers to. It was storming in my life and no matter what happened, I needed to lean on God.

When I flew back to Bama on Monday, I made the decision not to act as if my heart weren't still bleeding from the ending of my marriage. In counseling, I allowed the scars to get the air they needed. How many of us really understand that things covered up don't heal well? I fasted and prayed for myself and the young lady in Walter's life.

Around the end of March, I realized depression had closed in on me. I slept all the time. I didn't feel like going anywhere and was barely talking to anyone. I let my thoughts consume me. At the beginning of April, Dr.

Strength, Courage, and Wisdom —India Arie

Hamilton asked me why I wasn't telling those around me the truth about Walter. "Is it to protect him?"

"No. I'm protecting me." I already knew the questions people were going to have—"Why did you stay? Were you intimate with him after the first incident? Did you know who he cheated on you with? How could you ever love him again after the Craigslist ad?"—and I didn't feel like being exposed to a truth I wasn't ready to answer myself.

I finally uttered the words I'd been holding back for over a year. Why wasn't I good enough for him? The Bible says love is greater than hope and faith, so why wasn't mine sufficient for my husband? There was no public shaming on my part. I stayed! I cleaned his house, kept his biggest secret, and chose to love him when he didn't deserve it. Yet that wasn't enough. I was mad at him, but I was furious at myself. So many things ran through my head: *Maybe if I'd been more of this and less of that, he wouldn't have sought something I could never give him.* And because of it all, I ultimately failed again at marriage.

Dr. Hamilton saw that holding back the truth had begun to eat away at my soul. She made the suggestion that if I felt inclined to tell my truth, do it. Within twenty-four hours, I told three people. I felt better—lighter. Finally feeling free to talk, I dialed the person I loved more than anyone else: Mama. I felt a phone call wasn't the way to tell her, so I told her we needed to meet to talk. We agreed to link up that Sunday.

For about ten minutes, she tried to guess what it was about. "What did I do?"

"Nothing, Mama. I just need to talk to you face to face."

"Are you and Walter getting back together? If so, you are grown and this is your life."

I laughed and told her that was a subject she didn't ever have to worry about me discussing with her.

We met at a local Cracker Barrel to have dinner. I was strategic in making sure we met in a public place. After ordering our drinks, I told her it was finally time for me to tell her why the marriage ended. Instead of telling her, I took out my phone, pulled up the screenshot of the Craigslist ad, and handed the phone to her.

A few seconds later, she said, "Oh, no, Torrie!" and grabbed both my hands. She cried for ten minutes straight. "I can't believe you went through that without me!" I held back tears as Mama processed one of the greatest anguishes of my life.

Once the tears stopped flowing, we ordered dinner and I filled her in on everything that had happened. The funniest thing happened when I tried to explain why I hadn't initially told her everything about Walter. She waved her hand in the air and dismissed it with, "You know me, and I would have ended up in jail." We both chuckled heartily at the acknowledgement.

Right before we left the restaurant, Mama grabbed my hands and said, "You never stop amazing me, child! Is there anything you can't get through? I'm so proud of you, Torrie!" I had held my emotions together, but now I cried because her words meant everything to me. I could literally feel myself being healed from the inside out.

Strength, Courage, and Wisdom —India Arie

........∽..........

On June 2, I met the woman whose name I'd found on Walter's and my refrigerator. In April, I'd been in Tennessee and missed Pinky Promise, a small group meeting a couple of friends and I were a part of. Chrishauna called to let me know a new young lady named Kelly had joined them and she was convinced this Kelly was the same one dating Walter. Although it made sense, I wanted to get as far away from the situation as possible. I prayed that the truth be revealed to her if she was with him and that Walter would get his life together.

About six weeks later, after I told friends the real reason behind the demise of the marriage, Tara, who was friends with Kelly and me, revealed to Chrishauna that Kelly had been dating Walter but they'd broken up months before. At first, Tara didn't think it was necessary to tell Kelly why Walter and I divorced. A week later, Tara decided that, because of the possibility of reconciliation between Kelly and Walter, Kelly needed to know the truth. I told Tara to be careful and let her know that if Kelly had any questions, I'd be open to talking.

The next day, as I was getting ready to lie down for my after-church nap, I got a call from Tara. Kelly wanted to talk to me, so we decided to meet at a local restaurant. Once we sat down and got settled, I told her, "Fifty percent of what Walter told you was true, and the other fifty percent was a lie."

Kelly said, "Well, he said you were crazy."

"That's the truth," I replied.

We laughed. It definitely helped ease us into the conversation. I wasn't surprised by the things Walter had told Kelly about us. According to him, we'd grown apart and there was no infidelity. Kelly shared that they were looking at engagement rings when he and I had that huge argument in February. We'd been divorced a solid two months at that time. Everything had been good with them until I showed up at the house. My prayer for several weeks after the blowup was that he would feel convicted and leave Kelly alone. Two weeks after I went to the house, Walter broke up with Kelly through a text message.

I looked at Kelly in awe. This young woman was smart and a minister. Our personalities were so similar; it was scary. Looking at her was like looking at myself with a different face.

In that moment, I was frightened as well. If I hadn't shown up at the house, Walter would have done the same thing to Kelly that he'd done to me. To think that I was so miserable for weeks after that altercation and three and a half months later, I find out it was a divine interruption for both Kelly and me. Because I'd felt inclined to clean the house for potential buyers, Kelly was no longer on the path to marriage with Walter.

As for me, I was required to say the things I could barely whisper to myself and I began to heal on another level. Many times, our breakthrough is on the other side of the very things we fear to face the most. None of us ever want to feel out of control of our lives or unworthy. When we dig deeper, we heal deeper.

Strength, Courage, and Wisdom —India Arie

Kelly and I had no idea that through tears and failed relationships, such a beautiful friendship would form. God was repeatedly showing me that not just some but all things can truly work together for our good if we give the pieces back to Him.

My woes with Walter deepened that summer when he moved to another state and put renters in the house without talking it over with me. I was truly learning that forgiveness isn't a one-time confession; it's a daily calling to make a conscious decision to forgive in spite of everything.

When that argument flowed over to another, I had to look beyond the surface. What was my problem? The house represented everything I desired and the reality of another dream shattered. It symbolized stability, safety, love, rest, and family. I'd barely experienced any of those things living there, yet my soul was still tied to what could have been. Life was teaching me that soul ties aren't just with human beings but things as well. I felt as if I were losing. But in time, I gained strength and peace of mind. Those two things are priceless. Though warranted, I had to give up my anger and right to be right. They weren't worth the head space or the energy.

Soon after that, Mama told me she'd be at my next Beloved meeting. Mama had attended Beloved once the year before, but that meeting was an open discussion night, so she'd never heard me speak. Now we were barely able to fit in Jenn's living room, but we were making it work. Mama's best friend Marietta decided to come too, and I was excited they would get the full experience.

The entire time I was speaking, they both cried so much that I couldn't even look in their direction. The presence of the Holy Spirit lingered throughout the house, and we could feel Him at work in each of us.

During the altar call, Tanya called me over and asked me to cover her as she prayed with Mama. It took me a few seconds to realize Mama was giving her life to Christ. Later that night, at my apartment, I asked Mama why she'd never done it before now. She responded, "I was always too scared to walk up to the front of the church by myself."

In that moment, I was at a loss for words. I figured that at some point during her journey she'd professed with her mouth and believed in her heart that Christ was her Savior. She hadn't. This was a prime example to me that assumption is dangerous. I made a vow with God not to ask others if they are saved but if they are far away from Him.

Beloved would be two in November, and I was already trying to figure out what we were going to do for the anniversary. I jokingly told a couple of friends not to be surprised if such and such well-known speaker walked into the house. After some thought and prayer, I reached out to Heather Lindsey, the founder of Pinky Promise, to speak at the anniversary. We communicated back and forth a few times before scheduling a conference call. During the call, we confirmed the date and details. I was beyond elated.

Strength, Courage, and Wisdom —India Arie

Later that afternoon, Mama called to chat. Our conversation had been a little stiff due to an argument we'd a couple of weeks earlier, but we were trying to make amends. She was upset. Life was plain hard for her, and she felt helpless.

"Torrie, I opened my Bible and I just don't understand it. And to be honest, what I read didn't help."

"Do you know what book you read?"

"I don't know. I just flipped it open and started there."

I explained to her that she needed to read according to the situation she was facing. "You can Google Scriptures for encouragement or depression.'"

Mama then admitted to dealing with guilt. "I'll never forgive myself for how I treated you and your sister growing up, especially for what I said to you. I think about it every day, Torrie. Don't you understand? That's why I covet you and Jessica so much!"

As she sobbed, I silently cried and cradled my phone. On the outside, Mama was this self-assured woman. On the inside, she was fighting a never-ending war with the hardest person to forgive: herself. We can ask for forgiveness for anything, but once words are spoken, you can't take them back. Mama didn't know anything about surrendering or trusting God. Throughout the years, the only person she knew how to depend on was herself. Walking in this newfound faith was hard, and she had no idea where to start.

"I've forgiven you, Mama. Now you've got to forgive yourself so that you can heal and move on."

"I'll never forgive myself. Ever."

I prayed with her and promised to send her a book to help her find what she needed in the Word. I couldn't get off the phone with her until her tears subsided. Mine, however, continued long after our conversation was over. I'd been trying to help Mama change for years, but God revealed to me that I'd taken on a task that wasn't mine to bear. He then showed me that while I was trying my best to change her, He was trying to do a work in me. My job was to love her and point in the direction of the cross. It's love, not our selfish ambition to fix people for whatever reason we've come up with, that draws people to repentance. By simply loving her, she would see God in and beyond me. I had to take the advice I'd been preaching to her: surrender. She was my mother, not some project. God promised me He would provide the words when they needed to be spoken and the restraint when I needed to stay silent.

Mama wasn't the only person God was showing me how to navigate. Walter had recently written me an email apologizing about what had happened in our marriage. Not too long before, we were going back and forth about his actions with the house and the divorce settlement. I was numb to his words, so I printed out the email and took it to my next session with Dr. Hamilton. She advised me to really reflect before responding and told me he was open to hear my response since he'd initiated the conversation.

At the end of August, I attended MegaFest, a huge festival put on by T. D. Jakes Ministries. During one of the sessions, I felt myself being truly healed from the anguish and pain the failed relationship had caused. My last night in Dallas, I sat down and responded to Walter's email. I told him what I thought, how I felt, and where I'd failed him.

During a panel that weekend, Shannon Tanner made a profound statement about emasculating the men in our lives: "We clip their wings and get mad when they don't wanna fly anymore." This was what I'd done, not just throughout my relationship with Walter but in previous relationships as well. I knew the seed had been planted during my childhood and watered throughout the years. I hadn't been patient or kind. How I felt ruled my world. I had been a complete bully to Walter. Just as he was seeking forgiveness, I wanted it too. I forgave Walter and then I forgave myself.

When I hit the send button, I knew I'd embarked on a new season. Everything was falling into place once again.

CHAPTER SIXTEEN

Meant to Be —TLC

I entered September fueled as never before. Closure, purpose, forgiveness, and peace will do that for you. I was seeing that as I elevated internally, so did every other aspect of my life, especially Beloved. We experienced our first physical healing, breakthroughs kept manifesting, and women were stepping into their destinies.

Before we knew it, November had rolled around and Beloved's anniversary event had arrived. I sought God earnestly about what to share, and He led me to Ezekiel 37. After giving me the title of the message, He told me to share about what had happened in Walter's and my marriage.

It's one thing to share something with a room of thirty women; it's another to tell strangers about something so personal. So of course, I fought God on it. After a couple of days, the Holy Spirit said, "You don't want to go without Me." It was a struggle to put my emotions aside and tackle the task, but I pushed through.

The anniversary event was a success, with a few hundred women showing up. Heather and Marquita, the worship leader, did an amazing job. My fear of being picked apart was replaced by strength, love, and so much encouragement. The women were incredibly loving. They thanked me for sharing something so personal and although their situations weren't the same as mine, they felt inspired. God was definitely doing a new thing.

Then came November 20. It started out like any other day. I got up and went about my routine as I prepared for work. On my break, I called and wished my daddy a happy fiftieth birthday. During lunch, I went to the gym in my building to talk to my friend Kaleiah, one of my fellow Zumba instructors. As we were taking, she asked when I'd last talked to Mama. I told her it had been a few weeks but I'd tried calling her over the weekend and didn't get an answer. I called Mama's number after our conversation, and it went straight to her voicemail, as it had two days before. Worry stirred in my stomach.

I texted Jessica, asking her when she'd last heard from Mama. After looking through her phone, she responded, "November 9 was the last time I heard anything from her." That was two weeks ago. I told her to go check on her before she went to work that night, and she agreed. After several minutes, she texted back, "I'm scared."

I reassured her that everything was fine and Mama probably was in one of her moods and didn't feel like being bothered. "Call me when you get there and I'll be on the phone with you when you go in," I said.

Twenty-five minutes later, Jessica called me after arriving at Mama's. Mama's car was there, and I advised Jessica to knock before she went in because Mama didn't like people showing up unannounced. She knocked a couple of times with no answer. After trying one key to get into the house, she went back to the car to get another key. "I'm in," Jessica said. She opened the door and took a few steps in. Something told me to ask her what it smelled like, but I dismissed the thought as soon as it came.

A few seconds later, Jessica screamed, "Oh, Mama, no!" With just those three words, I knew Mama was dead.

I barely remember dropping my phone or stumbling out of my desk. I don't remember when I fell on the floor or who carried me to the empty office. I do remember that first breath after hearing Jessica scream and the unmentionable ache that engulfed every fiber of my being. I wept.

The tears subsided long enough for me to ask someone to go get my phone. Jessica was hysterical, and I could hear chaos in the background as neighbors and family arrived after finding out the news. She calmed enough to say, "Torrie, please hurry up." I shook off the shock so I could get to her as soon as possible.

As Jenn and Marquita drove, they called my friends to let them know what had happened. As protocol, the police had to question Jessica about what happened, so I went to meet her at the station when I finally arrived in Wetumpka. The world stood still for a few moments after I laid my eyes on her. When we were little, I used to hate any part of her touching me because we just didn't get along.

But at that moment, I'd never been so relieved to have her in my arms. She could have stayed in them forever.

Our lives had been permanently changed. Had I suspected anything, I would never have sent her to that house. From that day forward, the image of Mama lying on that floor would be etched into Jessica's head, and there was nothing I could do to erase it.

The police spoke briefly with me to let me know that because Mama wasn't dressed and the house was in a bit of disarray, they had to secure the house with crime scene tap. They promised to work quickly to find out the cause of her death and notify us immediately.

After hugging family members and friends at the station, we headed over to my aunt Clockie's. Clockie lived on the street in front of Mama's. More family and friends arrived and gathered around us. Texts and phone calls flooded my phone, but my sole focus was Jessica. She was a wreck.

After a while, people began to leave. I decided Jessica and I would drive back to Birmingham so I could get some clothes besides the ones on my back. We promised to let everyone know when we made it safely.

As I started returning calls, I noticed Walter had called several times. When he answered, I went off on a tangent about November 20 being the worst day ever made. "The only thing decent about it is that it's Daddy's birthday. I've forgiven you, but today will forever be known as Doom's Day! I'm going to write President Obama and ask if he can take today off the calendar. That way we can go straight from the nineteenth to the twenty-first."

"Torrie, I didn't call about us. I called to check on you because I heard about your mom."

"We found my mama dead, and two years ago on this date, I found out you were cheating on me."

Silence. The weight of the moment settled before Walter responded with an apology. He asked if he could call and check on me the next day, and I told him that was fine.

Jessica and I drove up 65 North hand in hand with faint music in the background. When we arrived at my place, I made sure she was settled, hoping she would get a little rest. I called my girlfriends, and we talked until sleep overcame me. Everything had changed that day in a matter of moments. My mama was gone. We had no idea how and would never know why. Before I drifted off to sleep, I prayed that my day was a really bad dream.

The next day, I ran some much-needed errands and did everything I could to comfort Jessica before heading back to Wetumpka. She'd barely slept the night before and neither had I. On the way back, the officer overseeing Mama's case called to let us know a stroke had ended her life. He agreed to meet us at the house to clear off the tape so we could get things in order for her burial. I hadn't suspected foul play, but it was a relief to know for sure she hadn't been harmed. After clearing everything outside the house, the officer went in and covered the place where Mama had been found.

Once the funeral home received her body, we were told based on the decomposition that she'd probably been dead at least a week, maybe longer. We were all dumbfounded.

For the next few days, friends helped Jessica and me get Mama's house organized. Walter wanted to make sure I was okay, so he came to visit as well. He arrived in town late in the evening, and when he got ready to leave to go get a hotel room, it was early in the morning. I told him that wasn't necessary and he was welcome to stay with us.

After grabbing his bag out of the car and taking a shower, he settled on the couch and I sat in a chair across from him. Walter caught me up on his life and I did the same. He then apologized for what happened while we were married, and I apologized for my shortcomings as well. A couple of months before, you couldn't have told me we would ever share time together again, especially under the circumstances. Our words were genuine, and I was grateful healing had taken place. Peace permeated throughout the room. This forgiveness was on a level I'd never experienced before.

I knew those around me wondered how I could allow Walter to be around me at a time like that. At the end of the day, he'd been my husband. Before things went left with us, he'd loved Mama and Mama had loved him. I didn't have the strength to even put up a fight with him, nor did I want to. My mama was no longer breathing. That, not Walter's presence, had my focus and thoughts. Hate is an awfully heavy emotion to carry around, and I needed love and support.

When we went to view the body days later, I initially couldn't cry. Mama didn't look anything like herself. Her face was swollen beyond recognition. My subconscious decided the woman lying in the casket wasn't my mother.

Jessica lingered over the casket as deep sobs rocked her body. I sat on the front pew and allowed silent tears to fall with Daddy close to my side. It was only when my gaze fell on Mama's hands that I lost it. Those were definitely her hands. Daddy held me as I came to the realization that that body was without a doubt Mama.

Back in October, Mama had randomly texted me, "If anything happens to me, it will be a one-inch binder with Alabama on the front. . . . All of my business, insurance, and house is in it." Did she feel death was near? Why?

I didn't have time to process that during the day, but at night, it haunted me. She'd been through a lot of transition lately. She was unemployed and job hunting, her finances were shaky, and she was at odds with several people in her life. Mama was beyond stressed. I knew a stroke ultimately caused her death, but knowing all that I did, I felt as though she'd really died of a broken heart.

When I opened my eyes on November 26, the weather was a mere glimpse of what my insides felt like: gloomy and threatening to overflow. I brushed my teeth, washed my face, and put on the dress I was going to wear that day. Somehow I even managed to put on some makeup.

People dropped food off and swaddled us in warm hugs. Shortly after ten, most of our family pressed their way into Mama's living room to pray before heading to the church.

In the family limousine on the way to the church, I couldn't look at Clockie. She was barely holding it together, and her face said more than I cared to admit in that moment. We made small talk and quieted as we pulled up to the church.

The night before, I'd called Kelly and asked her to make corsages for the immediate family. She walked up as we entered the foyer and began putting them on us. The pastors officiating the service lined up in front of us. There was nothing left for me to do, nothing to distract me from what was about to take place.

We began to walk behind the pastors as they recited Psalm 23. I looked into the eyes of one of Jessica's friends and felt her sadness, remorse, pity, and genuine concern shift something inside me. When I was little, Mama would fall asleep in the room while I was up playing or watching TV. If her breaths were too quiet, I would stick my finger under her nose to make sure she was still breathing. Her next breath made me realize I'd been holding my own in the hope that hers hadn't stopped. How was I supposed to go on, knowing I would never feel her exhale again?

In that moment, time stood still as it sank in that this was the last walk I would take to lay eyes on my mama. The night before, I'd spent time writing a card to put in her casket. Now I laid the card near her head. I kissed the face of the one person who I knew loved me more than life itself and whispered in her ear how much my heart already missed her. Nobody told me time could speed by and stop at the same time. I'm convinced a hole in the shape of her formed in my heart as I took one final glance at her. When I took my seat, I pressed my palm into my Daddy's hand even harder and began to cry the saddest tears of my life.

While family and friends continued to view Mama's body, Marquita began to sing the lyrics from "The Anthem":

> *Hallelujah!*
> *You have won the victory.*
> *Hallelujah!*
> *You have won it all for me.*
> *Death could not hold you down.*
> *You are the risen king!*
> *Seated in majesty,*
> *You are the risen king.*

As I closed my eyes, the words soaked into my spirit. In that moment, I knew that even though blood was no longer running warm through Mama's veins, God still got the victory. Did it make sense? No. But it was well with my soul.

I got up and spoke for a few minutes during the service. I shared how Mama had accepted Jesus as her Savior five months before her death and told them not to let her lying in her casket at the altar be in vain. I reminded them that we always think we have tomorrow, next Sunday, or next year, but none of that is promised to us. I urged everyone to get right with God before they left the building.

That night, after everyone left, my thoughts competed with the rain drumming on the roof. I once heard that if it rains on the day of a funeral, the deceased person's soul had gone to heaven. I tossed and turned, praying that the sound of the rain would dull the ache in my chest. At some point, sleep found me.

I'm almost sure we were still in shock on Thanksgiving as we managed our grief almost frighteningly well. The fact that a meal was being prepared in Mama's house on her favorite holiday but she wouldn't even get to smell it was beyond foreign to me. We received so many texts and calls that day. The thoughtfulness of everyone who reached out to us no doubt carried us more than we'll ever know on this side.

I returned to Birmingham the next day, but not without lingering like a mother leaving her baby at daycare for the first time. Would Jessica be okay? Would I miss some major paperwork being delivered? Mama had built that house from the ground up; I knew how hard she'd worked to give us a place to call home. And the fact that it was the place where she'd taken her last breath made me feel as if I were leaving her. Jessica assured me by reminding me we were a call away and a ninety-minute drive from each other.

My thirtieth birthday was on December 1, and I continuously glanced at my phone, willing Mama to call. Several times throughout the day, I sat on my couch and listened to voicemails she'd left. Most were from her pocket dialing me, but some were her talking or going off on me.

I was just happy to have something—anything—with her voice on it.

Hours turned into days and days turned into weeks. Many nights, Jessica and I fell asleep on the phone listening to each other's cries. Normally, I couldn't find sleep with any lights on, but I often found myself waking up with at least one light on. Night didn't seem to last so long with light filling the darkness in the room.

My weight was dropping noticeably. Marquita was the first to say something. I told her I could eat if food was in front of me, but I honestly didn't have the energy to prepare food. She took me grocery shopping and then spent hours in the kitchen making food for me.

Several other friends came over and just kept me company. I resumed counseling and cried at work, in the car, or wherever. No place was off limits.

Before I knew it, it was New Year's Eve. I went to a church service in Atlanta with some of my girls. That day, I kept my composure; but as midnight neared, I lost all reservations. 2013 would be the last year I'd laid my eyes on the queen of my heart. I didn't want to transition into another year without Mama, but there was nothing I could do to stop it.

The only thing constant in life is change. In literally one minute, everything can go from cosmos to chaos and vice versa. How could 365 days revolutionize so many things in my world? The year went from worst to best and then from best to worst.

While sitting in that service, I took a good look at my life and how God had kept me in every moment. I finally understood when more seasoned people said, "I'm so glad to be in my right mind!" Just the thought of not being in a straitjacket in a padded room brought fresh, humbling tears to my eyes.

I wasn't sure about what 2014 would bring, who would exit it with me, what I would face, or if I'd sum the year up as great. All I did know was that if all else faded, my Savior was true and faithful to me. As I glanced at my phone to see whether midnight had passed, I knew that somehow, no matter what, I'd make it.

EPILOGUE

Bruised but Not Broken —*Joss Stone*

While soothing the ache of the breakup with my college sweetheart in spring 2007, I listened to music to help ease the pain, as usual. The first time I heard Joss Stone's lyrics croon through my speakers, her words took up permanent residence in my soul. The song spoke life to me.

As she always did whenever something major was going on in my life, Mama stopped everything in her world to come check on me. Over lunch a few days after the breakup, she told me if any person ever took the light out of my eyes, she'd kill them herself. Although it was dim, she claimed to see a small twinkle so no one was going to get hurt. Wink!

No matter what came my way, light illuminated my vision. For many years I thought that light was pure resilience and strength. Later, I realized the light was actually God. Even when I didn't know Him or accept His Son, He made sure I had a glimmer of hope through everything life handed me.

None of us gets though life without internal bruises. Sometimes you walk away from situations with physical ones. Bruises are a little tricky. Many times, they look worse before they heal. They may even be sore to the touch and unpleasant on the eyes. Like most injuries, they heal from within before they show improvement on the outside. The beautiful thing about bruises is that eventually they fade away.

Acknowledgements

Jesus Christ—You are the love I searched for all of my life. In You I've found purpose and been made whole.

Thank you, God, for sending Your one and only Son to die for a wretch like me.

To my daddy, Darryl—God is a restorer of time and all things. Thank you for showing me that love conquers the past, the present, and the future. You are one of the most vital pieces to my puzzle. It's an honor to be your arrow. Psalm 127:3–4. I'll love you and honor you until the end of time.

Jennifer—Thank you for loving us and making my daddy a better man.

Devan and DJ—I'm so lucky to be your sister! Nothing is greater than love, and through it all, it's what holds us together!

Riley, Baby Landon, Summer, Ashton, and SK—Your auntie, big cousin, and sister hopes that if I slay my own personal dragons, you won't have to fight half of what I did. You five have been more of an inspiration than you'll ever know!

Arrie Bell, Emmitt, Betty, Reubena and Carey, my amazing grandparents who gave the gift called family—Thank you from the bottom of my heart.

La Familia! Bridgette—You are one of the most selfless people I have ever known! You will always be the Queen B of my heart! Ashley—You were my first friend and confidant. No matter what road life leads us on, I know I can always count on you. Polly, Mary, Gail, Clockie, Elgie, Kat, Kim, Shyla, Shan, Brenda, Ann, Kathy, Faye, Bruce, Broderick, Big Toot, Mook, Cody, Greg, Larry, Walter, and Bunk—All of you have been instrumental in my journey.

Kristen—It's been twenty-five years since we first laid eyes on one another. I used to be amazed at how well we know each other, but the realization that I am you and you are me settled in my spirit as I typed this. I know I'll never have to face anything this world throws at me alone, regardless of how many miles we are apart. My tears, joys, accomplishments, and failures haven't been my own; they've been yours too, and vice versa. Absolutely no one else in this world can say half of what you say to me and make me laugh the best laugh of my day. I know your heart. In fact, both of ours have the same rhythm. Thank you for holding my hand through the last two decades, allowing me to evolve, and reassuring me that my existence was meaningful in those moments I was so unsure of myself. We are them Fi-Fi Cha'man guhs! "We made a deal ages ago. Men, babies, it doesn't matter. We are soulmates!" —SATC2

Toni—Thank you for being not just a friend but a sister. I'm indebted to you for typing up 100,000 words because my computer skills are awful! "You and me, us never part!" Facts, not fiction!

Chrishauna, Holly, Krispin, Alicia, Ashley Talley, Marquita, Misha, Baby T, Toya, Rosetta, Abihail, Jenn—My circle. My secret keepers. My shoulders to cry on. My encouragers. My friends. I am a reflection of all of the good in you. Thank you for believing in me.

Benkie, Juanica, Lakerri, Freddy—Thank you for being there every time I've needed you through the years.

Ashley Joy Sutton—Your presence in my life has propelled me forward to be the best version of Torrie I can be while staying true to my core. Love you so much, sister fran. Thank you for everything!

Ashlee, Antwain, Ashley Flores—You all have added so much value to my life! I thank God for having such great friends in ministry! Thank you for all the advice, phone calls, and impromptu texts and for talking me off several ledges and helping me to truly believe in the impossible.

To my spiritual mama, Tanya—Thank you. Thank you. Thank you. You didn't birth me, but you have loved me as if you did. It's an honor to be your daughter in the Spirit! Your grace and loving arms have infected not only me but also a generation of God's people. I'm so excited to see what he has in store for you! Proverbs 31:29.

Dr. Patricia Hamilton—You brought me back to life! I will never stop singing your praises as one of the most essential reasons why I was able to get my life together. Counseling is so much more than your profession; it is your purpose. I'm still sad you aren't stateside anymore, but I know the nations are healing through your beautiful gift!

A sincere thanks to all of the spiritual leaders in my life: Pastors Arthur Smith, Scott and Pat Schatzline, Sean and Enid Cherry, Jon Potter, and Jeremy Saylor—Your influence and faithfulness to the call on your lives has challenged me in ways you'll never know.

My Zumba fam—Your influence compelled me to find the rhythm of my heart! Special thanks to Kaleiah, Tiffany Hood, and Tiffany Moore. To my sweet students—You all are the BEST part of my day. Each of you is so special to me!

Micah and Shed—Why the both of you have sown so freely and faithfully into Beloved is beyond me! I'm so thankful for your obedience, sacrifice, support, advice, and friendship. "Internationally known, locally recognized!" LOL!

Demetrius and Mr. Robert—You both have been more like family than coworkers. Thank you for encouraging me and being sounding boards for each and every transition I've been through since we've worked together.

Stephen—Thank you for being an amazing friend and challenging me in the fourth quarter to keep pushing!

Acknowledgements

Beloved's Dream Team—I could go on for days about you all. I see servanthood, destiny, and purpose all over each of you! Thank you for being the heartbeat of Beloved and allowing me to serve beside you!

The Lambda Zeta chapter of Delta Sigma Theta—Y'all are some of the most driven, hardworking women I know! It's an honor to call you all my sisters! Shout out to the forty-six Visions of R.A.D.I.A.N.C.E.! Oo-Oop! #LZMade

If you have been a part of my life in any moment (whether virtually or in person), added value, or revealed the healed or bruised parts of me, thank you for motivating me to be better than I was the day before.

Permissions

Chapter Nine, page 48

"Imagine Me" (Kirk Franklin): Copyright © 2005 Aunt Gertrude Music Publishing Llc. (BMI) Bridge Building Music (BMI) (adm. at CapitolCMGPublishing.com). All rights reserved. Used by permission.

Chapter Sixteen, page 91

"The Anthem" (Henry Seely, Joth Hunt, Liz Webber): Copyright © 2008 Integrity Worship Music (ASCAP) Planet Shakers Ministries International Inc. (APRA) (adm. at CapitolCMGPublishing.com). All rights reserved. Used by permission.

Note

[1] Definition of "Beloved" compiled from Google Definitions. *https://www.google.com/search?q=+Beloved+Definition&ie=utf-8&oe=utf-8*

Made in the USA
Charleston, SC
08 July 2016